A matter of choice?

Explaining national variation in teenage abortion and motherhood

Ellie Lee, Steve Clements, Roger Ingham and Nicole Stone

JR JOSEPH ROWNTREE FOUNDATION 1904 2004

The **Joseph Rowntree Foundation** has supported this project as part of its programme of research and innovative development projects, which it hopes will be of value to policy makers, practitioners and service users. The facts presented and views expressed in this report are, however, those of the authors and not necessarily those of the Foundation.

Joseph Rowntree Foundation, The Homestead, 40 Water End, York YO30 6WP   Website: www.jrf.org.uk

Research Team
Roger Ingham, Ellie Lee, Steve Clements, Nicole Stone, Ian Diamond (until December 2002)

Researchers
Gerel Altankhuyag, Sarah Ball, Martyn Brooks, Beccy Bundock, Liza Renyard, Judith Ruddock, Helen Taylor

Advisory Group
Mary Boyle, Dilys Cossey, Ann Furedi, Rachel Garbutt, Alison Hadley, Ian Jones, David Paintin, Gillian Penney

JRF Research Manager
Charlie Lloyd

JRF Policy and Practice Development Manager
Maggie Jones

© University of Southampton 2004

First published 2004 by the Joseph Rowntree Foundation

A CIP catalogue record for this report is available from the British Library.

ISBN 1 85935 181 6   (paperback)
ISBN 1 85935 182 4   (pdf: available at www.jrf.org.uk)

Cover design by Adkins Design

Prepared and printed by:
York Publishing Services Ltd
64 Hallfield Road
Layerthorpe
York YO31 7ZQ
Tel: 01904 430033; Fax: 01904 430868; Website: www.yps-publishing.co.uk

Further copies of this report, or any other JRF publication, can be obtained either from the JRF website (www.jrf.org.uk/ bookshop/) or from our distributor, York Publishing Services Ltd, at the above address.

Contents

The Centre for Sexual Health Research

The Centre for Sexual Health Research, University of Southampton
http://www.socstats.soton.ac.uk/cshr

The Centre for Sexual Health Research is a multidisciplinary research team involving researchers from a range of disciplines including psychology, social statistics, sociology, social policy, demography, geography, public health and others. The aims of the Centre are to provide a focus for research related to issues of sexual health; to encourage and develop high quality interdisciplinary research, using both quantitative and qualitative methods; and to provide a local, national and international resource on issues relating to research and policy formulation.

Ellie Lee is Lecturer in Social Policy at Kent University. Between 2001 and 2003, she was Research Fellow at the University of Southampton, working with the Centre for Sexual Health Research. Her PhD, awarded by the Women's Studies Centre at Kent University, is about the abortion debate, and she is the author of books and papers about this issue.

Steve Clements is a Research Fellow in the School of Social Sciences at the University of Southampton. He has worked with the Centre for Sexual Health Research for a number of years researching teenage sexual health in the UK and reproductive health in the developing world. His PhD, awarded by Southampton University, examined the geographic variation in teenage conception rates and conception outcomes in Great Britain.

Roger Ingham is Reader in Health and Community Psychology, and Director of the Centre for Sexual Health Research at the University of Southampton. He has been actively involved in research into young people's sexual conduct for many years, in the UK and abroad. He has been a consultant for the WHO, was a member of the core group to develop an integrated sexual health and HIV national strategy for England, and is a member of the Independent Advisory Group of the Teenage Pregnancy Unit.

Nicole Stone has worked as a Research Fellow at the Centre for Sexual Health Research at the University of Southampton since 1995 leading and co-ordinating a variety of projects in both the UK and internationally. She is currently working towards her PhD into the contraceptive and service use dynamics of young people.

Acknowledgements

- All those who completed questionnaires (Phase Two site teenage pregnancy co-ordinators, hospital O and G consultants, local commissioners and Phase Three site general practitioners).

- All those who were interviewed in Phase Three sites.

- Many others who helped along the way in providing data, access, administrative support, etc.

- Staff at the Joseph Rowntree Foundation.

- Members of the Advisory Group.

1 Investigating abortion proportions

For every young person, the pathway from sexual initiation to parenthood involves a sequence of choices ... Whether consciously or unconsciously, actively or passively, all adolescents make choices about their sexual and fertility behavior.
(National Research Council, 1987, p. 27)

Background and overview

Why do some young women who find themselves pregnant continue the pregnancy, while others opt for abortion? What factors shape the ways young women experience pregnancy and make decisions for or against abortion? These are the questions that this research project addresses.

As the quotation above rightly indicates, there is a sequence of points at which young people, more or less consciously, make choices that have implications for their fertility. In Great Britain, however, the point at which abortion decisions are taken has been granted considerably less attention than have other points along this pathway. Recent government policy documents addressing teenage pregnancy and sexual health say relatively little about abortion (Social Exclusion Unit, 1999; Department of Health, 2001). They do not dwell much on the question of why pregnant young women might choose or reject abortion, and they also say relatively little about abortion services and how they might be improved. Most policy initiatives have focused on other 'choice points', primarily before conception (addressing sexual activity and contraceptive use) and following childbirth (addressing teenage parenthood). The question of why pregnancies are aborted or continued, and what young women's experiences are in this regard, are thus worthwhile subjects for research.

Examination of these issues needs to be set in historical context. As Table 1 shows, numbers of teenage conceptions have reduced markedly over the past 30 years, and the *abortion proportion* (the percentage of teenage conceptions that end in an abortion) has increased (as, indeed, it has for women of all ages).

Young women are now therefore less likely to get pregnant and less likely to have a baby than they were 30 years ago. One particularly interesting aspect of this trend, however, is the degree of *variation* that exists between areas in relation to abortion proportions. For England and Wales, the 1999 to 2001 data for *under 18* conceptions (under 18 figures are not published for Scotland) reveal that, overall, 44 per cent of these ended in an abortion, with this figure ranging from 18 per cent in Derwentside, County Durham to 76 per cent in Eden, Cumbria. This variation shows that there is a lack of uniformity in the choices being made by teenage women in regard to abortion.

Table 1 Teenage conception and abortion measures in England and Wales, 1972–2000

Year	Numbers of teenage conceptions (1,000s)	Numbers of teenage abortions (1,000s)	Abortion proportions
1972	130.6	27.7	21
1982	113.9	36.9	32
1992	93.4	31.6	34
2000	97.7	38.4	39

Source: ONS Birth Statistics Series FM1, Table 12.1; Wellings and Kane, 1999.

The research described in this report was designed to provide some insights into *this specific issue* – the variation in abortion proportions – as well as exploring the decision process more generally.

There are difficulties associated with much discussion of *teenage pregnancy*. The existence of a 'problem' associated with fertility in women in their teenage years has too often been assumed rather than substantiated (Phoenix, 1991; Macintyre and Cunningham-Burley, 1993); as the latter authors argue, 'it is simply taken for granted that conceptions (or births or abortions) occurring in the teenage years are problematic'.

The authors of this study are very aware of this problem, and have made no *a priori* assumptions about whether pregnancies occurring to women aged under 18 years are necessarily a problem, either for 'society' or for the individuals concerned. Neither does this study aim to suggest that there is an 'ideal' abortion proportion, or that policy makers should attempt to achieve uniformity in outcomes of conceptions. However, the existence of the wide variations noted above strongly suggests that there *are* issues that policy might usefully address.

Before moving to describe the design of the research project, the results of which are reported in the pages that follow, the report briefly outlines the way that abortion is currently provided in Britain to provide further context for the discussion.

Abortion provision in Britain

Under British law, a pregnancy can be legally terminated where two doctors agree – indicated by their signing a form from the Department of Health – that the circumstances of the pregnancy match one of the criteria specified in the 1967 Abortion Act (as amended by the 1990 Human Fertilisation and Embryology Act). For the purposes of this study, the most important criterion is that which states that an abortion can be performed because the continuation of the pregnancy constitutes a greater threat to the physical or mental health of the pregnant woman than does its termination. Abortion can be legally performed under this ground up to 24 weeks of pregnancy, and it is under this ground that the majority of abortions at all ages are provided in Britain.

Unlike maternity services, it has not been the case that women who have abortions have been automatically entitled to NHS-funded services. NHS funding for abortion has varied considerably across Britain ever since it was legalised in 1967 (from 90 per cent in some places to less than 50 per cent in others in the 1990s) and the reason for this variation has been put down to the existence of differing local criteria (Abortion Law Reform Association, 1997, 1999). Although such criteria have generally been abolished over the past two or three years, funding disparities still exist.

In this context, women seeking abortion normally go through three stages: the referral stage (the point at which they request that a doctor refer them to an abortion provider), the consultation (where they discuss their request and other relevant issues with an abortion provider) and the procedure itself.

Referral

General practitioners (GPs) are the most frequently used first port of call for women, including young women, seeking abortion (Allen, 1990; Marie Stopes International, 1999).

A basic issue with regard to GP referral for abortion is the availability of GPs. The accessibility of abortion may, in some instances, be affected by difficulty of access to GP surgeries, especially in rural districts in which a number of branch GP surgeries have recently been closed (Countryside Agency, 2000). GPs' attitudes to abortion referrals are another key issue. Reluctance among some GPs to authorise abortion requests has, for many years, been highlighted as a potential problem for women seeking to terminate a pregnancy (Lane Committee,

1974; British Pregnancy Advisory Service, 1978; Sheldon, 1997). Recent research suggests, however, that GPs are generally sympathetic to young women's abortion requests and are not likely to perceive pregnant teenagers as a group 'undeserving' of NHS-funded abortions (Abortion Law Reform Association, 1997, 1999; Marie Stopes International, 1999).

The growth of family planning and sexual health services, and the encouragement of the need to pay special attention to young people in this context, is a significant development of recent years (Wellings and Kane, 1999). Such services should refer young women for abortion under the terms of the abortion law and are expected to do so in a supportive manner, although there is evidence that this is not always the case (Allen, 1990; Harden and Ogden, 1999).

There have been in recent years a number of specific innovations that aim to make it simpler for young women to be referred for an abortion consultation. These include 'signposting' of services (involving more proactive advertising, especially of telephone numbers of referring agencies) and central booking systems (where all women locally access abortion services via one specialised agency that concentrates specifically on booking consultations with abortion providers). No published data are available to date that report the extent to which teenage referrals have been influenced by these initiatives.

Consultation and procedure

Following discussion with the referring doctor, women are booked in for an appointment for consultation with an abortion provider, who will then arrange the procedure if the decision is taken to proceed. Abortion providers in Britain are NHS hospitals (usually gynaecology departments), specialist independent providers of abortion services (bpas, Marie Stopes clinics, and a small number of other clinics) and private hospitals. NHS units, and British Pregnancy Advisory Service and

Marie Stopes clinics provide the vast majority of abortions, although in Scotland non-NHS provision is minimal.

The need to improve abortion provision has been highlighted in some recent policy documents. The Royal College of Obstetricians and Gynaecologists deems abortion to be an important aspect of women's health care, and has set targets for the waiting time between referral and consultation, and consultation and procedure, which providers are supposed to meet. These state that the maximum waiting time in each case should be 14 days with a maximum of a three-week wait in total, but ideally waiting time would be less (Royal College of Obstetricians and Gynaecologists, 2000). It has also set out best practice guidelines for providers to follow (Royal College of Obstetricians and Gynaecologists, 1991, 2000). UK government policy demands that NHS trusts ensure that abortion services are adequate to meet local need (Department of Health, 2001), and Royal College of Obstetricians and Gynaecologists (RCOG) targets have been endorsed. Reducing waiting times has again been emphasised very recently as a target for abortion services, and medical abortion (use of the 'abortion pill' for abortions at early stages of pregnancy) promoted to assist targets to be met (Stationery Office, 2003).

A significant recent development is the increased role of specialist providers, rather than NHS hospitals, to provide NHS-funded abortions. British Pregnancy Advisory Service (bpas) and Marie Stopes clinics provide abortion procedures paid for by women themselves but, in recent years, they have increasingly provided NHS-funded procedures (where the abortion is funded by the NHS but provided by bpas or Marie Stopes clinics). The balance between NHS-funded procedures provided by these organisations, and procedures provided by NHS hospitals, varies from area to area. In Scotland, abortion is almost entirely NHS funded and NHS provided. In England and Wales, there is a great deal of variation, with some NHS trusts providing services through NHS hospitals alone, some through contracted specialist providers only and some by using a mix of modes of provision (for example, NHS hospitals providing abortion to women from the locality at early gestations and bpas at later gestations). This development in abortion services raises a range of issues – thus far unexplored by research – about the potential impact of variations in the accessibility and quality of abortion provision.

A summary of previous findings on abortion proportions

All British women are currently provided with abortion in this context but, as noted previously, the proportions of conceptions to under-18s that end in abortion vary considerably across Britain. Relevant research published to date indicates that there are some relationships between abortion proportions and the following indices.

Social deprivation

Social deprivation, where it features in existing research about abortion proportions, is a broadly drawn category including parents' income, social class (as measured by parental occupation), educational level, health status and employment status of young women. Social deprivation has been highlighted as having a strong influence on conception outcomes as well as on conception rates.

The proportion of conceptions that ends in abortion has been shown in a number of studies to correlate with some indices of deprivation in geographical areas,[1] such as local authorities. More deprived areas are associated with higher teenage conception rates as well as with higher proportions of these conceptions ending in maternity (Wilson *et al.*, 1992; Garlick *et al.*, 1993; Social Exclusion Unit, 1999).

Correlations obtained between deprivation in areas and outcomes of conceptions may be wrongly extrapolated to individuals, giving the misleading impression that there is no differentiation between what individuals, living in the same area, do. As a result, some studies have measured the relationship between deprivation and conception outcomes in smaller sized areas, such as postcode areas; the relationship with deprivation still pertains. Conception has been found to be six times more frequent among teenagers from deprived, as opposed to affluent, postcode areas, with two-thirds of teenage conceptions terminated in the latter kind of areas and only a quarter terminated in the former (Smith, 1993).[2] Other research has found a similar correlation (McLeod, 2001).

Where research has focused on individuals, deprivation has also been found to be related to conception outcome. In a logistic regression analysis of 269 pregnant teenagers in West Glamorgan, those opting for a maternity were more likely, at the time of conception, to be living in overcrowded households and less likely to be in full-time education (Lo *et al.*, 1994). Moore and Rosenthal, in their review of data from the UK, argue that:

> ... teenage abortees are more likely than those who carry their pregnancies to full-term to be contraceptive users, single, have high educational status or occupational aspirations, and to be of high socioeconomic status.
> (Moore and Rosenthal, 1993, p. 151)

Access to abortion

There is little evidence in Britain to show that the variation in teenage conception outcomes is related to the variation in the provision of terminations (Wilson *et al.*, 1992), although there has been relatively little detailed research regarding this issue. One study found that significant variation remains in abortion proportions between health authorities after accounting for ward-level social deprivation, which may suggest that service availability is an issue (Diamond *et al.*, 1999).

Related research has found that more extensive provision of youth-oriented family planning services is associated with higher proportions of under-16 conceptions being terminated (Clements, 2002).

Interpersonal variables

Male partners' responses to a pregnancy influence whether or not the pregnancy is continued (Tabberer *et al.*, 2000), and the relationship with the partner has also been shown to be important in terms of outcomes (Henderson, 1999). Those with planned as well as unplanned pregnancies who opt to continue to maternity are more likely to be married or cohabiting (Pearson *et al.*, 1995). These factors would contribute in a major way to regional variations in the proportion of conceptions ending in abortion only if there was geographic variation in the relationship status of teenage women. This may be the case but, if so, is possibly connected to other variables – for example, educational attainment – that may in themselves be related to the age at which young people marry or form stable unions.

Parental influence over conception outcomes has been investigated in mainly qualitative terms. Some research suggests that, where teenagers opt for abortion, their parents may not have been influential because they may not have been consulted; this may be because negative responses to the news of pregnancy (primarily disappointment) are often anticipated (Ooms, 1981; Harden and Ogden, 1999; Pope *et al.*, 2001). Research involving young women who continue a pregnancy suggests that abortion is rarely discussed in families (Tabberer *et al.*, 2000). It has been argued that, where parents are 'supportive' and 'non-judgemental' in their response to news of a pregnancy, this can be interpreted as a sanction to continue, not an endorsement of the option of abortion (Allen and Bourke-Dowling, 1998). The relationship between whether and how pregnancies are discussed in families, and

variations in abortion proportions, has not, however, been investigated quantitatively, probably because of the obvious difficulties involved in collecting such data.

Qualitative approaches have also been used to explore the influence of friends and other community members in pregnancy decisions. Attention has been drawn to how decisions are influenced by social networks (with young women generally making similar decisions to those of their friends and others in their communities) and by the relative visibility of early motherhood (Burghes, 1995; Whitehead, 2001). These phenomena may best be considered, as with the influence of partners and parents, to be components of a broader process shaping the ways interpersonal relationships develop and influence behaviour (Luker, 1996).

The research project

The overall research aim was to investigate the relationship between the factors described above and abortion proportions among women aged 17 years and under. The specific stated aims at the outset were to:

- explore, through statistical analyses, the ways in which demographic and socio-economic factors are associated with abortion proportions

- explore the statistical relations between aspects of service provision and abortion proportions

- explore the perceived and actual barriers to accessing abortion services and opportunities for change

- investigate and identify the various contextual factors that impinge on young people's decisions regarding motherhood and abortion

- integrate the different data sources to account for variations in abortion proportions in England, Wales and Scotland.

The research comprised three phases.[3] Those who wish to follow the details of the statistical approaches used, or to find out more about other specific components of the research, can do so by obtaining the detailed Technical Report, which is available on request.[4]

Phase One

The aim of this phase was to develop a 'map' of the whole of Britain (England, Scotland and Wales), indicating the relationship between abortion proportions and other factors for which data are available for this geographical spread. Since the Office for National Statistics publishes national data on abortion proportions by local authorities (the lower tier[5] of official administrative units), all data were analysed for the same geographical areas. Overall, the analysis considers evidence from 406 local authorities in Great Britain (352 in England, 22 in Wales and 32 in Scotland). Abortion proportions for 1997–99 were used since these were the latest available data at the start of the study. Combined figures over a three-year period were used to obtain reliable statistics, because for some local authorities the annual absolute number of conceptions is low, and year-by-year variation is relatively large.

Data collection

A range of demographic and socio-economic indices, data regarding abortion services, and figures for conceptions and conception outcomes was collated (as detailed in Appendix 1, Table A1.1). Owing to the organisation of statistical data offices in the UK, some data had to be obtained from more than one source. Consequently, it was not always possible to collect exactly the same information for local authorities in England, Wales and Scotland. However, every effort was made to obtain data as closely matched as possible.[6]

Data analysis

An initial exploratory analysis investigated the association between under-18 abortion proportions and each potential explanatory factor. Statistical modelling methods (logistic regression)[7] were employed in order to identify the extent to which the various potential explanatory factors (alone and/or in combination) were associated with the variation in abortion proportions.

Phase Two

While local authorities vary greatly in their overall abortion proportion, there are also wide variations *within* them. Phase Two aimed to take into account this variation. The advantage of this approach is to minimise any false impressions that can be created where associations in areas as a whole are incorrectly implied as associations that would apply for individuals, as discussed above. Furthermore, restricting these analyses to a smaller number of local authorities enabled the collection of many more potential explanatory factors that were not available nationally or that would have been too time-consuming to include in Phase One.

Procedure for site selection

Twenty-one sites (18 from England and Wales, and three from Scotland) were selected in order to provide a sufficient number of conceptions to perform the analyses, and to enable detailed examination of a range of social deprivation and service provision conditions. They were randomly selected within ranges of conception rates and abortion proportions (see the Technical Report for further details).[8]

Data collection/preparation

In order to perform the necessary analyses, individual conception data were required for the 21 sites. For reasons of confidentiality, it is not possible to obtain the detailed annual conception and outcome data for England and Wales required for this analysis from the Office for National Statistics (ONS). Instead, these were collated from maternity records and abortion notifications, as detailed in the Technical Report. The final dataset contained 18,293 under-18 conceptions.

In relation to the potential explanatory factors, some local authority indicators collected for Phase One were used in this analysis (socio-economic and service provision data) along with census ward measures of deprivation and ethnicity, and local authority measures of abortion and referral service provision. These are detailed in Appendix 2 (Table A2.1).

Finally, questionnaires were distributed to teenage pregnancy co-ordinators, directors of service commissioning and hospital consultants in each of the 21 sites. Using the information collected, a panel of experts assigned scores to each site relating to a number of abortion provision indicators, as follows:

- the ability of the unit that provides abortion *in the site* to meet local demand for the service

- the availability of first trimester procedures (those in the first 12 weeks of pregnancy)

- the availability of procedures performed later in gestation

- the referral process quality, as a whole, for under-18s

- the access to NHS-funded procedures

- the specific supportive measures available for under-18s who terminate pregnancies

- the accessibility of TOP (termination of pregnancy) for under-18s overall.

Data analysis
The data were analysed using multilevel statistical models (multilevel logistic regression). The use of a multilevel model ensures that the hierarchical data structure (that is, individuals within census wards within local authority areas) is accounted for in

order to make the results statistically valid. It also has the advantage of identifying variation between the local authorities and wards, after accounting for significant explanatory factors, thus highlighting areas of unexplained variation.

Phase Three
This phase was focused on six of the 21 sites used in Phase Two, two with high abortion proportions (Wirral and Enfield), one medium (Swindon) and three with low proportions (Leeds, Norfolk and Bridgend). Its three components were as follows.

- Semi-structured interviews with young women who conceived while aged 17 or below, including those who terminated and those who continued their pregnancies. Three main themes were covered: the availability of abortion services and experiences of services generally, perceptions of abortion and influences on decision making.

- Semi-structured interviews with samples of older people in the sites in order to explore 'community' attitudes towards abortion.

- A survey of general practitioners in order to explore attitudes towards abortion, perceptions of local services and other relevant issues.

It should be stressed that the work in this phase was not intended to enable specific conclusions on these *particular* sites to be reached. The sites were selected as being typical of sites at different points along the continuum of abortion proportions; however, the necessarily low numbers of participants involved in qualitative approaches make any claims regarding representativeness of the samples very tenuous. Rather, the aim was to explore themes that may assist in understanding the processes involved in decisions for or against abortion.

Interviews with young women

Recruitment of young mothers was achieved through contact with local service providers and others. As with other previous studies in this area, it proved to be extremely difficult to recruit a large enough number of young women who had undergone terminations in each of these sites, despite extensive efforts through abortion service providers, sexual health services, word of mouth, snowballing and so on. The decision was therefore made to extend recruitment to other parts of the country; this achieved an eventual sample of 52 who continued and 51 who terminated their pregnancies, with all of the former category and 24 of the latter from within the six selected sites. Appendix 3 provides further details of the samples.

Interviews with older people

It had been hoped to interview some of the parents of the young women interviewed, but this proved impossible for practical and ethical reasons. In each site, a number of relevant local and community-based organisations were approached and participants were also recruited through snowballing. Priority was given to the areas within each site that were associated with higher numbers of teenage conceptions.

Survey of general practitioners

A survey of general practitioners in wards with a reasonable number of teenage pregnancies in each of the six sites was conducted, leading to a return of 175 completed questionnaires. Further details are available in the Technical Report.

Data analysis

The semi-structured interviews were transcribed verbatim and analysed to explore the key themes emerging on the topics of concern. The returns for the GP survey were unequal across sites, so were combined into two groups in order to ensure reasonable numbers in each. Bridgend, Leeds and Norfolk were combined to be the lower-proportion sites (all below 40 per cent) with Swindon, Enfield and Wirral being the higher-proportion sites (all above 40 per cent). This provided samples of 131 and 44 respectively.

These different aspects of the research project are summarised in Table 2.

The structure of this report

The research project, taken as a whole, thus ranged from the macro-level (involving national data on geographical patterning) through to the micro-level (involving intensive interviews with young women and older people in specific communities).

This report is organised thematically using three key themes, and the authors hope that this format will make the findings more accessible and will enable links to be made between the different levels of analysis of research findings that were adopted. Accordingly, the report is structured as follows.

Chapter Two discusses the issue of deprivation and its relation to pregnancy outcomes.

Chapter Three considers service provision and related aspects.

Chapter Four summarises the results in relation to interpersonal relationships and influences on decisions, and related issues.

Chapter Five brings the various strands together and considers the implications for policy.

In each chapter, the relevant statistical results are summarised, followed by summaries of the key themes to emerge from the qualitative analyses.

Table 2 Summary of phases, methods and samples

Detail	Phase One	Phase Two	Phase Three
Geographical coverage	England, Wales and Scotland	21 selected sites	Six selected sites
Units of analysis	406 lower-tier local authorities	1,412 wards within 21 local authorities	Local authorities
Measures used	Routine data on social deprivation, demographics, service provision and funding	Additional indicators of service provision and social deprivation	Interviews with 52 young mothers and 51 young women who experienced TOP
		Surveys of teenage pregnancy co-ordinators, health service commissioners and hospital consultants	Interviews with local community 'older people' Survey of 175 general practitioners
Methods of analysis	Logistic regression modelling of 141,849 conception outcomes	Multilevel logistic regression modelling of 18,293 conception outcomes	Thematic analyses of transcripts
		Construction and inclusion of service quality indicators	Analysis of questionnaire returns

2 Social deprivation and abortion proportions

This chapter explores the relationship between abortion proportions and social deprivation. The national picture is analysed in regard to abortion proportions and their statistical relationship to socio-economic factors. This is followed by a summary of the key results from the 21 sites selected for Phase Two, using more detailed measures. Finally, young women's accounts of their views about abortion, and how factors related to social disadvantage and advantage relate to their decisions about whether to end or continue a pregnancy, are explored.

The national picture

The data used in Phase One of this study related to the period from 1997 to 1999 inclusive. There were 141,849 under-18 conceptions in Great Britain – a rate of 45.8 per 1,000 women aged between 15 and 17 years.[1] Of these, 41 per cent were terminated. Women aged below 16 years were much more likely to terminate than were 16 and 17 year olds (51 per cent as against 39 per cent).

There was considerable variation in the under-18 abortion proportions, ranging from 69 per cent in Kensington and Chelsea to 25 per cent in Clackmannanshire, Merthyr Tydfil and the Shetland Islands. The distribution as a whole is shown in Map 1.

Deprivation indices
Under-18 abortion proportions were tested against a range of social deprivation measures.[2] For under-18s, there is a clear relationship with each of these measures (more affluent areas having higher abortion proportions), with the strongest relationship being obtained with the percentage of 11 to 15 year olds that are dependants of family credit claimants (r = –0.68). Table 3 shows the relationship between abortion proportions and quintiles of the numbers of children of family credit claimants.[3] Map 2 shows the distribution pattern in

Table 3 Relationship between numbers of dependants of family credit claimants (FCDs) and abortion proportions

FCD quintiles	Mean abortion proportions	Numbers of LAs	Standard deviation
1.00	54.2	60	6.9
2.00	49.4	84	6.5
3.00	44.0	99	6.9
4.00	39.3	78	6.3
5.00	35.8	85	6.7

Great Britain as a whole for abortion proportions, alongside that for dependants of family credit claimants. Under-16 abortion proportions are also correlated with the deprivation indicators, although not so strongly.

The ONS classification[4] also proved to be a strong predictor of the variation in abortion proportions. This association shows both a socio-economic and geographic divide. *Mining, manufacturing and industrial* areas have the lowest abortion proportions, while *Inner London* authorities have the highest (see Table 4).

When the deprivation measures were entered into the statistical model, the dependants of family credit claimants and the ONS classification, in combination, proved to be the best in accounting for the variation in abortion proportions.

Ethnicity
No ethnicity factors were statistically significant after accounting for deprivation. Comparing between different ethnic groups (defined using categories from the 1991 census), the African-Caribbean group correlated more strongly with a higher abortion proportion than did the Indian, Bangladeshi, Pakistani and white groups. However, in the vast majority of local authority areas, the non-white population is small in number, meaning that high correlations will not occur.[5]

Table 4 Mean under-18 abortion proportions for ONS classifications (*n* = 406)

ONS area classification	Means (standard deviations) of abortion proportions (%)	Number of local authorities
Inner London	55.6 (7.0)	11
Education Centres and Outer London	51.9 (6.7)	20
Prosperous England	51.1 (6.7)	82
Rural Areas	46.2 (7.9)	70
Urban Fringe	43.5 (7.1)	93
Coast and Services	40.1 (7.4)	51
Mining, Manufacturing and Industry	34.1 (4.7)	79

Unexplained variation

Social deprivation factors therefore accounted for the majority of the variation at the national level. However, significant unexplained local authority variation remains. Chapter 3 reports the extent to which this unexplained variation is due to factors relating to abortion service provision.

The local picture

Turning to the more detailed Phase Two study of the 21 sites, the data comprised 18,293 conceptions (10,790 maternities and 7,503 abortions), of which 3,391 occurred to young women aged under 16 years at conception. These represent approximately 13 per cent of all the under-18 conceptions that occurred in Great Britain between 1997 and 1999. The percentage of conceptions aborted in these study sites combined is 41 per cent, a figure that almost matches the national percentage at the time of the study (39 per cent), indicating that the selected sites are not atypical.

Variations in abortion proportions

The abortion proportions together with the under-18 conception rates for the Phase Two sites are shown in Table 5. The overall abortion proportion for under-16s is 49.7 per cent and 39.0 per cent for 16–17 year-olds. There is a very high correlation across sites (*c.*0.80) between the under-18 and under-16 proportions, although there are one or two notable exceptions.

Social deprivation

Of the 1,412 wards in the study sites, 978 are classified as urban, 247 rural fringe and 187 rural. Urban wards generally have lower abortion proportions, with 40 per cent overall, compared with 52 and 53 per cent in the rural fringe and rural wards respectively.

A number of more specific measures of deprivation were tested in the statistical model in this phase compared with Phase One.[6] Most showed that women were less likely to abort in more deprived areas and four distinct measures of ward-level deprivation were significant in the model, two of which are youth-specific. They are the percentage of:

- the economically active population who are unemployed
- 17 year olds not in full-time education
- 11–15 year olds who are dependants of family credit claimants
- residents aged under five.[7]

These factors substantially account for both the local authority and ward variation in abortion proportions. The inclusion of these deprivation measures in the statistical models also reduces the urban–rural differences discussed above to such an extent that these are no longer significant. This implies that urban–rural differences are primarily related to deprivation, with urban areas being more

Map 1 Under-18 abortion proportions in Great Britain

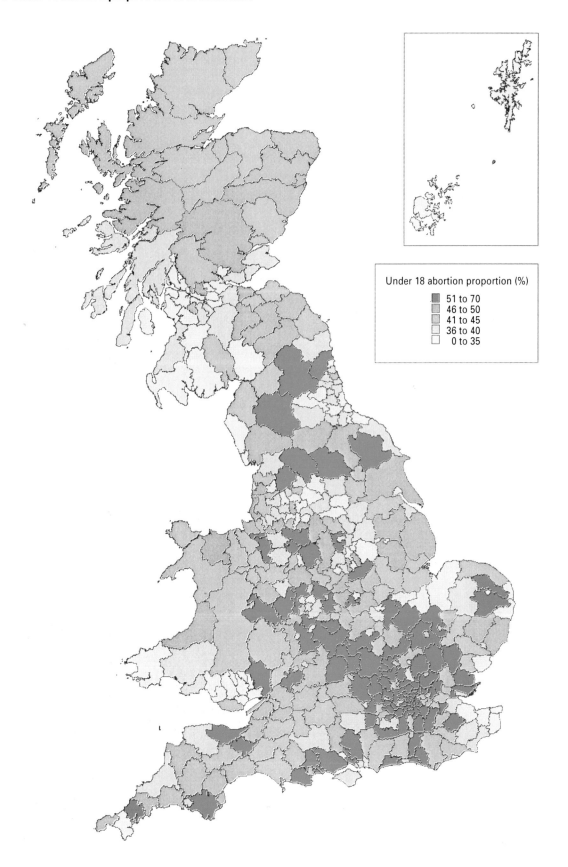

Under 18 abortion proportion (%)
- 51 to 70
- 46 to 50
- 41 to 45
- 36 to 40
- 0 to 35

Map 2 Distribution of dependants of family credit claimants

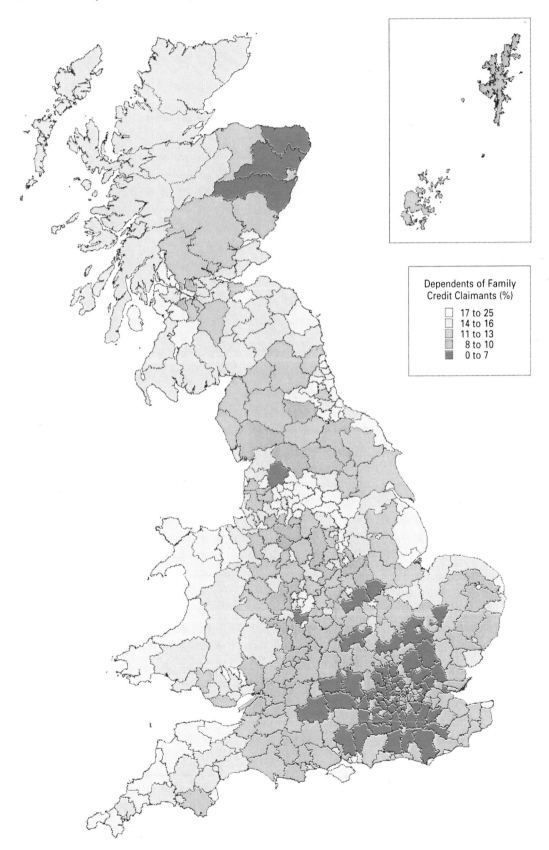

Dependents of Family
Credit Claimants (%)

☐ 17 to 25
☐ 14 to 16
☐ 11 to 13
☐ 8 to 10
☐ 0 to 7

Table 5 Conception rates among 15- to 17-year-old women, and under-16 and under-18 abortion proportions (in percentages) in the Phase Two sites

Site	Under-18 conception rates	Under-16 proportions	Under-18 proportions
Richmond-upon-Thames	21.8	68	64
Enfield	46.5	67	57
Lambeth	85.1	54	56
Islington	59.8	58	56
North Somerset	36.2	44	48
Wirral	46.9	61	47
Trafford	36.6	51	46
Greenwich	67.0	49	44
Cambridgeshire	29.6	53	44
Lincolnshire	43.9	55	42
Lothian	50.7	47	41
Swindon	56.1	49	40
Vale of Glamorgan	48.0	42	40
Leeds	52.6	50	38
Northumberland	43.2	52	38
Norfolk	38.7	53	38
Telford and Wrekin	61.6	50	37
Isle of Wight	40.4	36	36
Bridgend	61.7	43	32
Greater Glasgow	45.5	40	32
Ayrshire and Arran	40.9	40	30
National data	**45.8**	**50**	**39**

deprived. The relationship with deprivation also varies by age; only overall unemployment rate was a significant predictor of the under-16 abortion proportions in these study sites.

Therefore, the research at the local level further confirms the correlation between abortion proportions and social deprivation identified at the national level.

Ethnicity

Non-white ethnic groups are concentrated in a small number of wards in the 21 sites in Phase Two. In 78 per cent of wards, fewer than 1 per cent of the 13- to 17-year-old female population were of African-Caribbean origin. Similarly, in 80, 88 and 93 per cent of wards, fewer than 1 per cent of the female population were of Indian, Pakistani and Bangladeshi origin respectively.

Only the percentage of African-Caribbean females was significant in regard to variation in abortion proportions when added to the statistical model, after accounting for deprivation (with higher proportions in areas with higher percentages of African-Caribbean females). This may be due to the lower sample size of other ethnic groups. There is no evidence in the literature at the individual level to add weight to the assertion implied by this finding that African-Caribbeans are more likely to terminate pregnancies than other ethnic minority groups, and further research is required to investigate this issue.

Unexplained variation

The more detailed modelling in this phase has again highlighted the importance of social deprivation in accounting for the variation in abortion proportions. However, it has also shown that significant variation remains between the local authorities and between the wards. As the analysis in this phase is much more detailed and involves a much wider range of deprivation measures, it is unlikely that this remaining variation is due to unaccounted social deprivation; it is more likely to be explained by other factors.

After taking into account the site-specific demographic and socio-economic factors, some local authorities reveal abortion proportions that are *higher* or *lower than expected*. Those with *higher* than expected proportions are Wirral, Edinburgh, Enfield, East Lindsey (Lincolnshire), Richmond-upon-Thames, Breckland (Norfolk) and the Isle of Wight. Those with *lower* than expected proportions are Fenland (Cambridgeshire), Bridgend, Kings Lynn and West Norfolk, Norwich (Norfolk), South Cambridgeshire, Islington, Glasgow, East Renfrewshire, Trafford, West Lindsey (Lincolnshire) and South Lanarkshire.

Chapter 3 includes discussion of service factors that may account for this remaining variation.

Young women's views

The statistical models show that, at a national and local level, there is a strong association between social deprivation and abortion proportions. Areas that rate highly in regard to social deprivation also have higher conception rates, meaning that many young women from such areas will comprise a significant proportion of the total *number* of under-18 abortions. However, the research carried out for this study clearly shows they are *relatively less likely* to have an abortion than young women from areas that are not as socially deprived. The statistical research thus confirms the idea that abortion *proportions* and social deprivation are strongly correlated.

This tells us little about why this correlation occurs. What is the relationship between social deprivation and abortion proportions constituted in? Drawing on the Phase Three interviews with young women who had experienced a pregnancy, this chapter now turns to consider this issue.

This is a complicated connection to address through qualitative research, since people are unlikely to explain their very personal and private experiences, such as pregnancy, in relation to social phenomena like the degree of social deprivation in the area they live in. It is possible to address this issue through qualitative research, however, if close attention is paid to the way young women discuss and describe the relationship between their experiences of pregnancy and other aspects of their lives; for example, their life experience and their plans and views in regard to education, earning a living and so on. It is on this relationship that the remainder of this chapter primarily reflects.

The starting point for the discussion that follows, however, is the issue of *attitudes* to abortion. Other research has found that there is a relationship between the ways in which young women (and men) view abortion and socio-economic background. The Social Exclusion Unit, on the basis of its consultations on abortion, points out 'young people in more deprived areas appeared to disapprove strongly of abortion' (Social Exclusion Unit, 1999, p. 59), implying that part of the reason for variations in abortion proportions is because young people from particular backgrounds value abortion differently and, as a result, have contrasting approaches about whether it could be an acceptable option for them in the event of pregnancy. There is, it is suggested, a connection between the extent to which abortion is viewed negatively and the factors already highlighted in this chapter.

Respondents' attitudes to abortion are therefore discussed first, followed by the ways they described their own experiences of pregnancy, and decisions for or against abortion, in relation to other aspects of their lives. (Respondents who continued their pregnancy are labelled 'M' and those who had an abortion 'TOP'.)

Attitudes to abortion

Respondents were asked whether they had already formed opinions about abortion in advance of their own pregnancy and, if so, what they were. Around half of the total sample framed abortion in negative terms:

> It's like murdering someone isn't it, killing a baby …
> it's evil, you're killing a baby.
> (M34)

> I think it's cruel. Even … a 13 or 14 year old … would
> be selfish to kill a life … I think it's wicked.
> (M23)

> … it's like murder, it's a life, you're getting rid of a life
> … I don't agree with abortions.
> (M37)

A 'foetus-centred' perception of pregnancy is apparent in these comments. While more respondents who framed their opinions this way had continued their own pregnancy, it was notable that around one-quarter of those who went on to choose abortion used similar language:

> I've always said 'no it's not right' … you just don't
> want to kill a baby.
> (TOP38)

> I didn't think it were right … killing someone else …
> at the end of the day you're getting rid of another life.
> (TOP22)

> I always said I'd never, never go through an abortion
> and think it's wrong … I kind of thought of it as if you
> were killing someone.
> (TOP3)

This attitude towards abortion was also expressed where respondents explained they thought there was only a narrow range of instances when it might be acceptable; where, as one woman put it, there was an *actual reason*. As M7 explained, this could be, 'If they find out that there's something wrong with the baby … it's OK to have an abortion then'. For some, like M44, 'If you get

raped', abortion becomes justifiable. This interviewee stated, 'if that happened to me I don't think I could keep a baby'. These ways of conceptualising abortion also indicate a 'foetus-centred' rather than 'woman-centred' approach, in that the only circumstances in which abortion is construed as being justifiable are where the pregnancy is in some way out of the woman's control. In other instances, the woman is implicitly deemed responsible for ensuring the pregnancy continues to term.

In contrast, fewer interviewees (less than a half) indicated that the woman should be able to terminate a pregnancy because she perceived that to be best. TOP12 thought this approach was common sense. 'I always said it should be completely up to the mother … they're the person that's going to be going through it … [it is] utterly their decision.' But her view was unusual.

Others who expressed what can be considered 'woman-centred' views mostly did not put them forward as being common sense. Rather, they indicated that they had come to accept abortion as a result of a particular experience – interestingly, most often, an encounter with a proponent of anti-abortion views; for example, arguments against abortion made in Catholic schools or by pro-life organisations. M50 thus explained, in response to her experience of anti-abortion arguments made at her Catholic school, that, 'I think it's up to the person, no matter what religion they are they all have their own choice'.

Notably, as many who continued as who terminated pregnancies had become 'pro-choice' this way. However, some of the respondents who did not suggest they were opposed to abortion indicated that they held no particular opinions on the abortion issue in advance of their own pregnancy.

These findings indicate that the case for the 'right-to-choose' abortion exists in a relatively weak form as part of the cultural context in which young women's opinions about the abortion issue are generated.

The experience of pregnancy

It would be misplaced, however, to view negative attitudes to abortion as being deeply ingrained, or stable. This point is illustrated very clearly in the accounts of some respondents, who had considered abortion to be 'wrong' or 'like murder', but explained how they underwent a significant reconsideration of their opinions:

> I used to think of it as a person from day one ... my abortion just made me change my mind completely.
> (TOP48)

> I never used to be for abortion I used to be against it, but until you're in that situation you can't say.
> (TOP1)

This applied to almost as many of the respondents who *continued* as of those who ended their pregnancy. For the mothers who highlighted the transformation in their views, attention was commonly drawn to the reality of life as a mother. As M2 put it, 'It's changed now, now that I've been through it and seen how hard it is ... you don't really understand until you're in that position really'. M35 stated, similarly, 'Once you've been there you think twice about things and you don't want to bring another child into the world'. M43 put it down to her increasing experience of life as she got older: 'I thought "if you don't want to have a baby, you shouldn't have sex" ... as I've got older ... now I think it's just got to be your choice at the end of the day'.

This change in attitude suggests these respondents had experienced a contradiction between what they previously viewed, on the one hand, as the moral or right thing to do and, on the other hand, 'real life'. In the abstract, abortion might be viewed as 'wrong' but, when a pregnancy occurred, abortion emerged as a practical solution in a context in which having a baby may not have been appropriate.

This dichotomy between abstract morality and 'real life' was also expressed by those who

indicated they had come to view abortion to be 'wrong but the right thing to do' (Furedi, 1998):

> My opinion was ... how could anyone do that? ... but ... it happens and, you know, it's the right thing to do sometimes.
> (TOP26)

> Abortion to me was wrong unless it was in the right circumstances, like with her [a friend] ... that was the right thing to do.
> (M36)

The attitude that abortion is 'murder' or 'taking a life' does not appear to be a stable one, and actual behaviour cannot be reliably predicted on the basis of attitudes about abortion before a pregnancy has been experienced. How actual decisions were described will now be discussed in more detail. Emphasis is placed on respondents' commentaries about their perceptions of opportunities available to them in social terms.

Narratives of social disadvantage and advantage

Motherhood as an escape route

Half of the mothers accounted for *their* decision to continue the pregnancy in 'foetus-centred' terms. They explained they simply could not countenance having an abortion having become pregnant because it would be wrong:

> It was just the idea of an abortion ... it's like killing someone really, isn't it.
> (M13)

> Me personally, I wouldn't be able to do it ... it's killing basically and I wouldn't want to do that.
> (M24)

> I couldn't do that ... I just couldn't.
> (M9)

Others framed the 'wrongness' of abortion in relation to ideas about responsibility: 'I thought ... it's my fault I got pregnant' (M20). 'If you're old enough to have sex then you're old enough to handle the responsibility', explained M6, and M25 said, 'I thought I couldn't [have an abortion] because it was my responsibility … I'd got myself into it'.

Some such respondents came from backgrounds that featured irregular employment or unemployment, or that were marked by other kinds of insecurity and instability, and comments about these aspects of their lives littered their narratives. M42 experienced pregnancy as something that gave some direction to her life: 'I was not very happy, and just wandering about all the time'. M23 explained, of her experience as a mother, 'I'm just a better person all round … [it has] been the best thing that's ever happened to me … if I hadn't had the baby I'm sure I would've been in jail, I'm sure I would have'. For M10, being a mother seemed like a better option than the others available to her: 'She's [her baby] settled my life down. They're all off on drugs and drinking every night [her friends] … I can see if I didn't have her I'd have ended up going that way'. For M19, while the pregnancy did occur 'earlier than it should be', nonetheless, 'my life is better … my friends they were stupid. They'd just go to clubs, and do drugs and stuff'.

These accounts do reflect a context of socio-economic disadvantage. For these respondents, pregnancy and motherhood were presented as an escape route from a future characterised by lack of achievement and lack of direction. The prospect of motherhood provided some certainty in a life otherwise experienced as unstable and insecure.

More generally, however, there was a noticeable difference overall in the way in which the mothers, and those who terminated pregnancies, discussed the prospect of motherhood. Of those who expressed an opinion, mothers tended to consider it more desirable to have a baby before the age of 25 years; more than twice as many mothers felt this compared with those who terminated a pregnancy. By contrast, more respondents who had an abortion felt that it would be better to be 30 or over when they first had a baby. Perceptions of opportunities available in the future shaped their views about this.

I don't want a kid to ruin my life

This was very clearly the case for some of those who terminated a pregnancy:

> I knew straight away what I was going to do … even if it wasn't university I just wasn't ready and I wouldn't have wanted to … I don't want a kid to ruin my life.
> (TOP30)

> There was no question of me keeping it because I knew I was going to go to university … I didn't want a baby … I'd had a good education and I had a career path to go down, it was all laid out for me.
> (TOP34)

While they may not have thought about the *issue* of abortion prior to pregnancy, these respondents expressed decisiveness and clarity about *their choice* to have an abortion in the event of pregnancy. Some such respondents indicated that broader factors than their own feelings and views were at work, shaping their expectations and encouraging a particular life course. TOP34 noted that her future was 'all laid out for me'. With reference to the difference between her social background and that of other girls who grew up in the same area, another observed:

> I see some girls my age that have three kids now … but in my school no question, it was just like … you do it [have an abortion] get on with it.
> (TOP35)

Where these respondents made a case about what would be the 'best age' to have a child, there was a very clear recognition that for them it would be later in life, if at all:

> I would have said late 20s … but now I don't know 'cos now if I was to get pregnant in my late 20s I would have just started my career and it would mess the whole thing up … I want a househusband.
> (TOP30)

I was thinking in the 20s but now I would probably be thinking in the 30s.
(TOP33)

These observations are consistent with the trend whereby first childbirth happens increasingly later in women's lives, or not at all for growing numbers of women, especially those with a university education. Notable also, in regard to the issue of the *best age* to have a child, was the articulation by some of opinions about what was considered to be very much the *wrong time* to become a mother – namely, as a teenager – on the grounds that it would *ruin your life*.

I don't want to be an old mum

The examples above make an interesting comparison to the case made by some of those who continued pregnancies. While almost all indicated that they thought it was important to get an education and to work, motherhood featured as a central aspect of their visions of their future life, often with other things fitted around it. Education, clubbing, and work were often represented as things that are to be 'done' or 'got out of the way' before 'settling down'; for example:

> *I said I was going to have a baby when I was about 25 … it's just an age, you've had your teen years … gone clubbing, got a job and everything and then it's time to settle down.*
> (M21)

These accounts clearly differ from those of young women who decisively chose abortion; 'jobs' replace 'careers' and 'get my education' replaces 'going to university'.

Particularly striking, in many such cases, was the rejection of the prospect of being an *old mum*. Where relatively advantaged young women perceived teenage motherhood as highly undesirable, being a mum in one's 30s constituted a very negative prospect for some of those who opted to continue; for example:

If people want babies, I'm not being nasty but when they're older I mean, well, that's up to them.
(M42)

I don't want to be an old mum. If someone has a baby young that's down to them.
(M35)

The narratives of both groups of young women may sometimes constitute retrospective justifications of choices made. Nevertheless, some members of these two groups of young women situated motherhood and its place in the life course quite differently. It is also possible that the public debate about the 'problem' of teenage pregnancy shaped our respondents' narratives, generating contrasting positions about the merits of delaying childbearing.

Deciding wasn't easy

Opinion was not entirely polarised on the issue of the best age to have a child, with contrasts between those who continued, and those who terminated, their pregnancies. It was the case for some who opted to have an abortion, for example, that motherhood *was* already an important aspect of the way they envisaged their future life. But, on balance, the responsibility of motherhood was not one they could take on and they opted to end their pregnancy; for example:

> *I just thought I can't bring a child into the world at the moment 'cos I ain't working, I'm still at home and I've got no support or nothing.*
> (TOP43)

In contrast to those who found the decision to have an abortion 'easy', this group found it more difficult, and explained their decision-making process more in relation to their perceived inability to take *proper care* of a child at this point, than to their own educational and career development. The *responsible choice* for these young women was to terminate the pregnancy, rather than continue it.

Missing out?

The evidence discussed above suggests, in line with previous research, that young women reject or choose abortion because of forces that influence the way in which they look at their overall lives and futures (Plotnick, 1993; Henderson, 1999; Jewell *et al.*, 2000; Welsh *et al.*, 2001). This does not mean that the apparent relative weakness of 'woman-centred' ideas about abortion is an unimportant factor, but the choices young women actually make about pregnancy cannot be separated from the ways in which the place of motherhood in their future life are perceived. Outcomes of conception are related to the degree of social disadvantage or social advantage and the perceptions of future lives that emerge as a result. However, it is necessary to add a note of caution in relation to the implications of this observation.

The relationship between socio-economic background and patterns of childbearing does not mean that those who view early pregnancy and motherhood favourably consider that they have necessarily 'missed out'. Previous qualitative research has found that young mothers often (although not always) are very happy with their choice, despite frequently lacking material resources, because they greatly enjoy being a mother (Phoenix, 1991; Luker, 1996). A recent review of US literature by Hoffman also noted that dire warnings about the effects of teenage motherhood for individuals and society may overstate or misrepresent the problems, and that some new research indicates that 'some of them [teenage mothers] end up doing rather well' (Hoffman, 1998, p. 236).

There is not space here to detail our findings about this issue, but it should be noted that many of our respondents, like those interviewed in other studies, did indeed perceive motherhood to have improved their lives:

If someone has a child it doesn't matter what age they are ... they say that you're only a kid yourself and you're too young ... but it's not how everyone says it is. It's good to be a mum ... it changes your life totally.
(M30)

People made out it ruins your life ... but I don't think it does ... I was expecting the worst but it wasn't half as difficult as I thought it would be. It's not now either. He's brilliant. [of her child]
(M25)

Chapter 2 summary points

1   Between 1997 and 1999, there was variation in under-18 abortion proportions at the local authority level, ranging from 69 to 25 per cent.

2   There is a strong correlation between abortion proportions and measures of social deprivation; areas that are more deprived have lower abortion proportions.

3   After accounting for social deprivation, no significant differences remain in regard to abortion proportions between rural and urban areas.

4   Young women's views about abortion frequently change once a pregnancy is experienced; for example, from being 'like murder' to 'the right thing to do'.

5   Young women's pregnancy decisions are dependent on economic and social contexts rather than abstract moral views.

6   Outcomes of conception are related to the degree of social disadvantage or social advantage and the perceptions of future lives that emerge as a result:

  •   continuing a pregnancy is more likely to be the outcome where life in the present seems in some way insecure and where it seems motherhood may 'change your life' in a positive way

  •   those who are certain that future life will develop through education and employment tend to opt for abortion.

7   Many young mothers report their experiences as being highly rewarding.

8   There is significant variation in abortion proportions that is not accounted for by social deprivation.

3 Abortion services

This chapter considers abortion services. Findings are discussed in three areas: the importance of provision of abortion services in relation to social deprivation in accounting for variation in abortion proportions; the referral process and its relationship to abortion proportions; and, finally, the effect of the quality of abortion services.

Abortion provision relative to other factors

Existing research about abortion proportions suggests that deprivation may outweigh issues relating to abortion provision (Smith, 1993). Phases One and Two used statistical modelling techniques to investigate this further. The study took into account the fact that the way abortion services are provided varies across areas; it varies in relation to the extent to which consultations and procedures are provided by NHS or independent providers.

The national picture
Independent providers (Marie Stopes clinics and bpas) that *perform* abortions are located in 17 (lower-tier) authorities in Britain, with a further 33 authorities having a bpas *referral* centre and/or a Marie Stopes advice centre (figures accurate at time of study).

Before taking into account social deprivation (that is, simply considering the statistical relationship between the nature of the abortion provision and variations in proportions), there is an apparent association between these indices. Authorities with a bpas or Marie Stopes clinic that *performs* abortions have slightly higher abortion proportions than those authorities without such

provision. There is no difference in abortion proportions between areas with dedicated *referral centres* and those without (see Table 6).

After deprivation has been controlled for, the association with abortion provision remains significant; in particular, the presence of a bpas clinic is related to higher abortion proportions.

In understanding this finding, it is important to consider the possible effect of the purposive placement of centres, where abortion services may be located in areas with high abortion proportions. The lower abortion proportions where there are only referral centres may reflect a targeting of areas of this kind. Discussion with those who have knowledge about the history of the development of these abortion services confirms this may be the case.

Abortion funding
Official statistics on the funding of abortions are reported under three categories: NHS (abortions funded and performed by the NHS), NHS-agency (where the abortion is funded by the NHS but performed in a non-NHS establishment) and non-NHS (where the abortion is privately funded and performed outside the NHS).

For Phase One of this study, measures of funding of both under-18 abortions and those for all women were obtained and compared to the under-18 abortion proportions for all local authority areas. The results indicate that, where there is more non-NHS provision, a higher proportion of conceptions are aborted while, where the NHS is the main provider, relatively fewer conceptions are aborted. Table 7 illustrates this relationship.

Table 6   Mean under-18 abortion proportions (in percentages) according to type of provision in local authority

Nature of provision	Means (and standard deviations) of abortion proportions	Numbers of authorities
bpas/Marie Stopes clinics	48.0 (8.9)	17
bpas/Marie Stopes referral centres	43.7 (9.6)	33
No specialist provision	43.8 (9.2)	356

Table 7   Relationship between percentages of all-age abortions provided by NHS and under-18 abortion proportions

Under-18 abortion proportion	Percentage (SD) of all-age abortions funded and provided by NHS
Low	76.3 (23.1)
Below average	64.8 (32.5)
Average	58.9 (31.3)
Above average	58.7 (30.2)
High	44.2 (26.8)

After deprivation is controlled for, the most significant aspect of abortion funding associated with the variation is the percentage of under-18 abortions funded *and* performed by the NHS. Local authorities where proportionately more abortions are non-NHS and NHS-agency provided have higher abortion proportions. This NHS funding factor remains significant even after Scottish local authorities are removed from the model (that is, those where there is very little non-NHS or NHS-agency provision).

The local picture

Abortion provision relative to other factors was considered in greater detail for the 21 sites examined in Phase Two.

During the study period, there were five independent abortion services operating in three of these sites; two Marie Stopes centres in Leeds, a Marie Stopes centre and a bpas clinic in Lambeth and a bpas clinic in Richmond-upon-Thames. Owing to the small number of centres, it was not possible to assess further the importance of this indicator.

However, data on other aspects of provision that were not available for analysis during Phase One were considered. These included the percentage of teenage abortions provided in early gestation, the ratio of teenage abortions provided during early gestation compared with those provided for older women (aged 25 to 29 years), the rate of NHS and all abortions actually performed in the local authority site itself and an indicator of met need (generated by comparing the number of abortions performed

within the local authority to the level of demand). Once added to the model, none of these indicators was significantly associated with the outcome of the pregnancies.

As with the national analysis, indicators of abortion funding were examined. Prior to controlling for other factors, they showed the same relationship as that obtained in Phase One; that is, areas with more NHS-agency and non-NHS funded procedures appear to have higher abortion proportions. However, after accounting for deprivation, *non-NHS funding* for all abortions (the extent to which privately funded abortions were performed on women of all ages resident in these areas) was the only significant factor predicting under-18 abortion proportions.

Overall, findings about funding suggest there is an association between abortion proportions and the prevalence of self-funded abortion, but there may also be other factors at work when there is independent-sector provision in a particular area that affect abortion proportions. It is possible, for example, that the visibility of abortion provision is increased where there is independent-sector provision and that this has an impact. Further research is required to investigate this issue thoroughly.

Abortion referrals

Data concerning referrals for abortion were collected in Phase Two, and in Phase Three through the survey of GPs and the interview study with young women.

Map 3 NHS funding and provision for under-18 abortions in Great Britain[1]

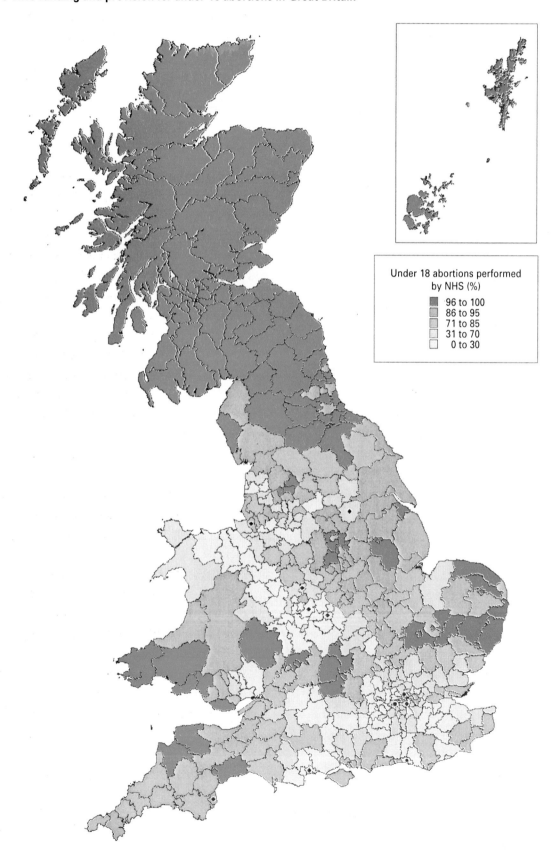

Under 18 abortions performed
by NHS (%)

- 96 to 100
- 86 to 95
- 71 to 85
- 31 to 70
- 0 to 30

Phase Two

A number of indicators were examined to assess the impact of referral service provision on abortion proportions.[2] No association was found between GP provision or characteristics of GPs at the *ward* level. This is possibly because this was measured by linking women to the GP surgery in their ward of residence.[3] However, it is likely that some young women will travel across ward boundaries to obtain sexual health services. Consequently, *local authority* based measures may more accurately assess the impact of local provision, particularly after accounting for variation in social deprivation within each local authority.

It was found that some local authority measures of referral services were associated with the outcome of the pregnancy, after accounting for deprivation. First, where there were proportionally more female GPs in a local authority, then there were higher abortion proportions. Second, where there was more family planning provision (where clinics were open for more days per week), then the abortion proportion was greater.

These factors markedly reduced the unexplained variation in abortion proportions noted in the previous chapter. Additionally, the non-NHS funding factor, discussed earlier, also becomes insignificant when these factors are taken into account. The key factor here was the adding of the family planning provision to the model. This implies that these two factors are correlated and it appears that the influence of more family planning provision is to increase referrals to non-NHS providers.

The influence of referral services also appears to vary by age. Among under-16s, the presence of more female GPs is not significant, but level of family planning provision is. This is consistent with published data reporting the greater use of non-GP services by under 16s (Seamark and Pereira Gray, 1996).

The final model can be seen in Appendix 2.

Phase Three: GP attitudes and practice

The GP survey in Phase Three aimed to assess if there were any correlations between reported attitudes and practice in the six sites selected, and abortion proportions. The survey did not highlight any significant relationships. The findings raise some other issues of interest, however, in regard to abortion provision currently.

Seventy per cent of respondents felt that referral routes were either good or very good. Only 2 per cent rated them as poor. In regard to their own practice, 89 per cent of GPs reported they did personally refer women aged under 18 for abortion. The vast majority of respondents agreed that NHS provision should be *always* available for under-18s who wish to terminate a pregnancy. Only 3 per cent thought that it should *never* be. Of the few who stated they did not refer, most stated it was because they conscientiously objected to abortion or the organisation of their practice did not require their involvement with abortion referral. These findings confirm those of previous research (Marie Stopes International, 1999) that GPs are generally very supportive of the provision of NHS-funded abortions.

Respondents were asked about their personal approach in regard to under-16 referrals, whether their practice had a written policy on confidentiality and, if so, whether it was advertised; results are shown in Table 8.

Notably, under two-thirds reported that they 'ever' refer under-16s without informing parents. Most of the explanations of the 'ambiguous' and 'qualified' responses referred to the Fraser guidelines,[4] even though the question asked about 'ever' referral as opposed to 'always'. The percentage reporting a written confidentiality policy is relatively low and, perhaps surprisingly, of those who do have such a policy, only two-thirds advertise its existence.

Table 8 Percentages of GP respondents who refer without informing carers, and who have confidentiality policies and who advertise them

Item	Response	%
Do you ever refer under-16s for abortions who refuse to inform their parents/guardians?	Yes	61
	No	13
	Ambiguous/ qualified response	26
	All	*100*
Does your GP practice have a written policy on confidentiality for young people, which says that under-16s may have the same right to confidentiality as older people?	Yes	43
	No	44
	Unsure	13
	All	*100*
If so, do you advertise your confidentiality policy?	Yes	67
	No	27
	Unsure	6
	All	*100*

Phase Three: young women's accounts of referrals

The interview study with young women, because it was qualitative, did not assess the statistical relationship between referral and variation in abortion proportions. Findings are reported because of what they indicate about the important issue of young women's experiences.

Who refers?

GPs were reported to be the most frequent referrers (accounting for 78 of 103 respondents' referrals); however, those seeking TOP were more likely to attend a family planning or sexual health clinic than those who continued their pregnancy. Fourteen of the 51 respondents who terminated their pregnancy were referred by a doctor at one of these clinics, compared with four of the 52 who continued. Respondents' narratives indicated clinics were perceived in a particular way:

> *They'll assume straight away that you want the papers for a termination ... I think it's nice for some people because ... [they] don't have to explain why [they] don't want a child.*
> (M35)

This example may relate to that reported above, that abortion proportions are related to family planning provision.

Barriers to abortion

The criteria of funding and referrers' practices showed that a small minority of respondents found the point of referral to be a barrier to accessing abortion.

Eight women who continued their pregnancies had, in fact, originally visited a doctor to request an abortion. In only one of these cases did the respondent indicate she decided to continue partly as a result of this appointment (the others simply changed their minds, or were affected by the scan at consultation, discussed below). This decision related to difficulties she perceived there to be, following the conversation with the doctor (at a family planning clinic), with having an abortion at 14 weeks' gestation. She did report that she would not definitely have had an abortion, however.

Two respondents discussed funding for abortion as being an issue, but both did terminate their pregnancy. One was a young woman who sought a referral from her local family planning clinic at 13 weeks' gestation. She stated that it had been made clear to her that it would be a lengthy and difficult process to get the procedure and, because of her gestational stage, it may prove to be the case she could not have had an abortion anyway. She added:

> *... they* [a family planning clinic doctor] *said it's really risky to do abortion because you might never have a baby again.*
> (TOP10)

In the end, she was 15 weeks' pregnant when she had the abortion and her boyfriend had to borrow from friends the £600 needed for a privately funded procedure. The other respondent indicated that there seemed to be various criteria used by the referring doctor as to whether TOP would be NHS funded, but that they did not apply in her case:

> *There was some sort of checklist ... he said, 'right we'll get it done' ... I think it was because of my age that I could get it free, otherwise I thought, 'God, I've got to pay £300'.*
> (TOP47)

Referrers' perceptions of abortion were also mentioned. In one case, the doctor (a GP) stated he was a conscientious objector, but the young woman was referred to another doctor in the same practice. Another GP, while not expressly indicating he disapproved of abortion, had tried to encourage continuing the pregnancy:

> *In my eyes he were more willing for me to have it and put it up for adoption ... I didn't like it ... I thought it were me who would make the decision, not him.*
> (TOP17)

More significant numerically (although small in absolute numbers) were cases where a health professional made it clear they disapproved of abortion. This was reported of one family planning clinic doctor, two GPs and two other staff members at a GP surgery; for example:

> *He was really horrible. He said that people who it's happened to, and it's not their fault, they should have priority. So I came out thinking that I couldn't have it done ... He shouldn't have been giving his opinion ... he should just look at everybody ... and help out with the best thing.*
> (TOP26)

On the other hand, a similar number of those who continued their pregnancy commented that it was the intention of the doctor to steer *towards* termination. This was experienced just as negatively as being steered against termination:

> *The doctor* [GP] *said to me, 'For girls of your age* [16] *we do advise termination'. My jaw hit the floor ... I was like no! ... You can't go round telling people to have terminations. It's up to them.*
> (M36)

Most, however, described the doctor's reaction to their pregnancy as being 'ambivalent' (that is, not steering towards one or other outcome).

Referral and decision making
About one-third of respondents went to a GP or clinic to request a pregnancy test. At this stage, some indicated they perceived seeing a doctor as an opportunity to discuss their options. Overall, the balance of accounts of this experience was negative. Staff taking insufficient time and care over explaining options was reported:

> [FP clinic] *He* [boyfriend] *said, 'Can we have the abortion sheets' ... I was just taken aback ... it would have helped if I was sitting in the room on my own ... I did go back to the family planning clinic and explained to the lady that I was keeping the baby.*
> (M1)

Most respondents indicated that the purpose of the initial appointment with a health professional was, in their minds, to obtain a referral rather than to discuss making a decision about what to do about their pregnancy, however. They had decided what they wanted to do *before* they saw a doctor. This was the case for 46 of the 52 respondents who terminated pregnancies. Of these, 14 still had some 'mixed feelings' about their pregnancy at the time when they visited the referrer, but nevertheless knew they wanted to request an abortion, while the remaining 32 had become very clear about what they had chosen to do in advance of the visit.

A negative feature of some such accounts was to feel 'over-counselled'. One respondent, for example, recounted:

> They asked [at the FP clinic] *why I didn't want the baby so I explained why not ... then she kept saying 'Are you sure? Are you sure?' ... she kept trying to push me ... I quizzed her, asked her 'why do you keep doing that?'.*
> (TOP25)

It would be wrong to conclude there was no perceived need for discussion with a referrer. On the contrary, discussion with a professional about the decision to terminate, and the practicalities of obtaining and undergoing an abortion, was perceived to be very important. As one typical respondent put it:

> I made my decision straight away. I didn't really need to think about it ... she [the GP] talked it over for a while with me so it was good.
> (TOP1)

This finding lends support to Allen's view (1990) that women seeking abortion can feel 'over-counselled', and that the main constructive role the referrer plays is not so much to introduce to women possibilities they had not already considered, but to make them feel supported and confident in whatever choice they had made.

Those who continued pregnancies similarly seldom described the meeting with the referrer as a time to simply discuss options. Only one of this group indicated that they definitely viewed the appointment this way. Three respondents did not

see a GP for referral at all because they presented straight to a hospital at a late stage in gestation. A further six said they were 'too late' for abortion to be an option. It was not in fact clearly the case that they were, but it was apparent from their narratives that they did not really see it as an option for them. Being 'too late' was the way they expressed this:

> She [GP] *gave me all the options ... either keep it or have a termination ... I was probably too far gone actually.*
> (M13)

This group overall had less to say about the referral process than those who were requesting abortion. This is likely to be related to the fact that those seeking abortion require decisive action on the part of the referrer, the actual mechanisms of which they were often unsure about; they therefore tended to discuss their experience in more detail at interview to illuminate the extent to which the doctor helped.

Perceptions of quality of referral process

Just under half of those referred for abortion rated the referrer positively (using terms 'good', 'helpful', 'nice', 'supportive', 'comfortable', 'options' and 'choice'), and one-fifth deemed them acceptable (using terms 'alright', 'fine' and 'okay'). One did not express an opinion, leaving about one-third who gave negative assessments (using terms 'horrible', 'bad', 'disgusting', 'crap' and 'awful'). Perceptions were less extreme on the part of those who continued, with 11 rating the referrer positively and exactly one-half as acceptable. One-fifth gave a negative assessment and five did not express an opinion.

Positive accounts featured discussion of the referrer being 'on the side' of the respondent. It was not endorsement of the particular choice that mattered so much as referrers 'respecting their right to make a choice' and 'being prepared to act on their behalf'. Typical comments were:

I think the family planning clinic is really excellent ... they're helpful, they don't presume things ... I suppose that's because they see young people everyday isn't it? So they aren't judgemental and they just try and help basically.
(TOP13)

He [GP] was actually very helpful, he mentioned all the places we could go, all the details, all the information we needed to know ... he gave us the whole lot.
(TOP40)

Those who used negative terms drew attention to the doctor being 'unhelpful' and appearing to be disinterested in their predicament.

Those who continued pregnancies perceived being assured they would be helped to get further care as less important, presumably because they assumed it would be available and accessible. The narratives of those who were positive about referral suggest that, in common with those who terminated pregnancies, it was respect for their right to choose that was most important, and there was sensitivity about this issue because of their age.

These findings are in line with those of other research, in particular that concerned with pre-abortion counselling. Indeed, the results provide a picture that is remarkably consistent with what has been known for almost 20 years. Allen, in her study of counselling in termination services, noted: 'there was evidence of a very functional approach by women to doctors ... Only 12 per cent said they went for a discussion on whether to have a termination or not' (Allen, 1985, p. 341). Boyle (1997) notes that her review of the relevant literature indicated women normally make up their mind *before* visiting a doctor, through discussion with those who are emotionally close, and Kumar and colleagues (2004) found that most women had made the decision to proceed with abortion before approaching the health service, and preferred not to discuss their decision, but expected non-judgemental support, information and prompt referral.

Interaction with the referring doctor is not perfunctory, however. There is a legal obligation to make sure the woman meets the terms set out in the Abortion Act, but the findings reported here suggest that, for women, the interaction with a health professional can constitute a significant part of their experience, for better or for worse. This is not because – for the majority – it constitutes a substantial aspect of the decision-making process; it is important for the reassurance and confidence it can provide and in allowing abortion to be *perceived* as a legitimate choice.

Quality of abortion services

Phase Two

Data on the perceived quality of abortion services were derived from the questionnaires completed by key informants as part of Phase Two for the 21 sites. As Chapter 1 explained, three questionnaire studies were carried out and the resulting data were rated by a group of experts along a number of dimensions.[5] The resulting scores were entered into the statistical models in this phase, to assess if service quality emerged as significant in explaining variations in abortion proportions. It is important to emphasise that this rating provided *relative* measures of quality; that is, the sites were scored in relation to each other, rather than in any absolute sense.

These ratings turned out not to be significant in relation to accounting for abortion proportions. As the overall accessibility score (the right-hand column in Table 9) indicates, there is no clear pattern linking the score to the abortion proportions in the sites. This suggests, for NHS-funded services at least,[6] that the quality of provision is not decisive for determining variation in abortion proportions.

Despite the lack of association between these ratings and abortion proportions, there were, however, important issues that emerged from the questionnaires about service quality.

Table 9 Expert ratings of selected quality dimensions for Phase Two sites (range from 1 to 5, with a higher score indicating higher quality)

Abortion proportion	Site	Ability to meet local demand	First trimester abortions	Post first trimester abortions	Overall accessibility score
Low	Ayrshire and Arran	4.0	4.0	2.0	4.0
	Bridgend	1.5	2.7	2.7	2.0
	Norfolk	3.5	3.7	2.3	3.7
	Northumberland	3.7	4.0	2.0	3.7
	Telford and Wrekin	1.3	2.0	1.7	2.0
	Leeds	3.0	3.0	2.3	2.7
	Isle of Wight	1.0	1.3	1.3	1.3
Medium	Cambridgeshire	3.3	4.0	2.0	2.7
	Greater Glasgow	3.7	3.7	2.7	3.3
	Greenwich	2.3	3.0	1.7	2.3
	Lincolnshire	3.0	3.0	2.0	2.7
	Swindon	1.0	2.0	2.0	2.0
	Trafford	1.0	2.7	1.7	1.7
	Vale of Glamorgan	2.3	2.3	1.7	2.0
High	Enfield	2.0	2.7	2.3	2.3
	Islington	2.3	2.7	2.3	2.3
	Lambeth	3.3	3.0	3.3	3.0
	Lothian	4.7	4.0	3.3	4.0
	North Somerset	2.0	3.0	2.3	2.3
	Richmond upon Thames	2.3	2.7	2.7	2.7
	Wirral	2.7	3.0	1.7	2.7

There was a commonly perceived problem of poor access to abortion after the first trimester, reflected in the almost uniformly low scores achieved by all sites (only Lambeth and Lothian scored above 3). While the legal time limit for abortions is 24 weeks (with the exception of where the woman's life is at risk, or where there is foetal abnormality), the highest cut-off point was 20 weeks. In most sites, it was reported that abortions are not provided in NHS hospitals from an earlier stage (between 13 and 16 weeks in most cases). Comments made by respondents indicated that, commonly, a 'division of labour' existed between NHS providers and bpas in this regard, with bpas providing these later terminations. There was recognition that this meant women had to travel some distance from their local area to get the procedure. In some sites, it also appeared that NHS units did not provide these procedures because of dislike among staff of involvement with abortion provision altogether.

Given that young women are relatively more likely to present later (Department of Health, 2003), this may be significant for the population group that is the subject of this study, although, because of the small numbers of abortions concerned, it would not affect variations in abortion proportions.

There were striking variations in the reported degree of support for providing abortion services within the NHS locally. No respondent indicated that there was significant *active* opposition to abortion provision, but the extent of reported positive support among health professionals varied significantly, especially among consultants. The following comments, taken from the questionnaire returns, provide some typical illustrations of this variation.[7]

Sites rated as high quality (all above 3.6 on five-point scale)

Nursing staff in TOP are very sympathetic and supportive. Consultants who do TOP see it as a sad but necessary part of their work ... consultants locally are sympathetic to the needs of young people.

[NHS staff are] comprehensive, sympathetic and helpful ... the service for [this area] and the surrounding area is easy to access and comprehensive.

All women of all ages should be provided with [an] NHS-funded procedure, preferably in dedicated clinics.

Two out of four [consultants] provide this service. Other staff 'opt' into the service. We have no difficulty in finding enough willing to take part.

Women under 18 get the same service as women over 18. [This area] has a long tradition of providing a reasonably efficient non-discriminatory abortion service.

A dedicated team of interested people of all grades delivers this service.

Sites rated as low on accessibility (all below 2.1 on five-point scale)

The situation is improving now. Before it was a lottery as to whether TOP was agreed. One consultant did not perform TOP for under-18s without parental consent. Some [doctors] make it very clear to women, especially under 18s,

(Continued)

that they do not agree with TOP provision as they were perceived as 'careless'.

Historically there have been no consultants willing to undertake the service. Where there has been one consultant s/he has still not offered the service ... because that consultant would then be under pressure of numbers ... there is no choice.

We have four consultants but only one will perform TOP ... [an] increasing number of O and G registrars are unwilling to undertake TOP.

The journey to bpas, is a 60-mile round trip. bpas holds the contract for NHS abortions for [in this area] ... very few abortions are carried out [locally].

There is a three to four week waiting time from initial referral to client's assessment appointment ... and only terminations under 13 weeks are carried out in the NHS.

NHS waiting time is too long, meaning we had to send some to bpas.

Phase Three: general practitioners' perceptions
GPs in the six Phase Three sites were asked for their views on the quality of abortion provision locally, and the findings were assessed in relation to the abortion proportion in the sites concerned.

Waiting times
Rather more respondents in the low-proportion sites reported shorter overall waiting times (a combination of 'under seven days' and 'between seven and 13 days') than in the high-proportion sites (32 per cent and 18 per cent respectively). In both categories of site, around 40 per cent reported 'between seven and 13 days' for both wait times (indicating a maximum time from referral to procedure of 26 days, just over the government target), and around 18 per cent

reported a combination of 'between seven and 13 days' and 'over 14 days'. Slightly higher combinations of '14 days and over' were reported from the high-proportion sites.

These results overall may suggest that pressure on services in the high-proportion sites leads to longer waiting times. Alternatively, the use of agency services may lead to longer waiting times for some reasons; for example, out-of-area provision. However, there were no clear differences on these measures between the high- and low-proportion sites.

Local modes of abortion provision
Table 10 shows that the pattern of provision varies somewhat, with more NHS-agency provision in the high-proportion sites; this applies to both first and second trimester procedures. The importance of independent provision for second trimester assessment is also clear from these data.

Perceptions of difficulties for young women are reported in Table 11. More marked variation is apparent for second trimester and post-20 week procedures. Respondents in the high-proportion sites report fewer problems for these procedures,

Table 10 Percentages of respondents who reported different routes of provision by category of site (multiple responses possible)

How do women aged under 18 obtain assessment for abortion in your area	Low proportion	High proportion
... in the first trimester?		
By referral to local NHS hospital unit	97	28
By referral to an NHS-funded service provided by an independent-sector provider	10	67
By referral to an independent provider whose fees they will pay themselves	11	8
... at 13 weeks' gestation and over?		
By referral to local NHS hospital unit	56	19
By referral to an NHS-funded service provided by an independent-sector provider	30	69
By referral to an independent provider whose fees they will pay themselves	40	14

Table 11 GPs' perceptions of local difficulties in abortion provision

Please indicate if, in your opinion, any of the following factors lead to difficulties for young women aged under the age of 18 in your area...	Response	Low proportion	High proportion
... difficulties in accessing NHS funded services in the first trimester	Yes	8	8
	No	89	78
	Unsure	4	14
... difficulties in accessing NHS funded services between 13 and 19 weeks	Yes	41	17
	No	40	61
	Unsure	19	22
... difficulties in accessing NHS funded services between 20 and 24 weeks	Yes	59	17
	No	18	31
	Unsure	23	51

again almost certainly because of the locality of independent providers. The high number of respondents who are 'unsure' of local processes probably results from them having little experience of these referrals.

Phase Three: young women's accounts

Quality of services was also assessed in Phase Three through the interviews with young women. It is not possible to relate these findings directly to statistical variations. They are important to report, however, because it may be the case that word of mouth in some areas does have an effect on local community perceptions of the available services and it is, of course, important for a study such as this to provide insights about young women's experiences.

Perceived adequacy of local provision in relation to demand

While no respondent reported that they had definitely continued a pregnancy because they could not get an abortion, travel problems were commented on where abortion at all gestations was provided on a contract basis and the provider clinic was located some distance away. One rated the actual care she got very highly, but noted:

> [It was] *miles away. I had to get the train ... I had to get about two trains, like change over at a certain place ... then a taxi from the train station to the actual abortion.*
> (TOP5)

Reported waiting times largely accorded with Royal College of Obstetricians and Gynaecologists (2000) recommended guidelines and confirmed the perceptions of GPs, noted above. The period between initial referral and the procedure was reported as being less than two weeks for two-thirds of respondents and over 30 days for 16 per cent. However, there was evidence that providers had to work very hard to make sure women got their appointments within the recommended time.

One woman commented of her local NHS unit:

> *Obviously it was very busy and they couldn't get me an appointment ... they actually found me a cancellation about two weeks after I initially came in.*
> (TOP11)

Another said 'it's hard to get an appointment because they're so packed' (TOP50) and drew the conclusion that there needed to be more clinics in her area.

There was also evidence of difficulties with local provision for second trimester procedures. As noted previously, problems in this regard were raised in accounts of referral, where referrers reportedly indicated that abortion might not be available because the pregnancy was over 12 weeks' gestation. In these cases, the referrer may have been misinformed about the local situation, but, in a few cases, it did seem that abortion after the first trimester was difficult to obtain locally. One reported that she was told:

> *I had to make my mind up because ... three months is the cut-off point ... the doctors don't like doing it or something.*
> (TOP13)

Another was referred at 13 weeks for an NHS-funded procedure at an independent clinic some miles away. She commented:

> *I really could have done without the hassle and the expense.*
> (TOP16)

Perceptions of service quality

There were strikingly uniform terms used by respondents where the experience of abortion services was positive. They talked about being treated in a *non-judgemental, caring* or *helpful* way, where having an abortion was viewed as *normal*, and being given plenty of *information* about what was happening. The following extracts illustrate typical accounts of this kind of experience.

Examples of positive experiences

[NHS agency] [of consultation] *They had a laugh with you, made you feel comfortable, it was just a really good environment. I wouldn't mind living there with them really ... that's how it should be, a big change from the other clinic [FP clinic where she went for pregnancy test] ... [of procedure] even though they see it every day ... they were still, as if to say, they loved their job and they were still helpful ... they know how you should feel and they were so helpful, it was just really good.*
(TOP40)

[NHS agency] [of consultation] *Everyone there was really, really helpful ... she had a chat with me, told me what the procedures were and gave me all these leaflets on day care and after care and what was actually involved and what I'd need to take with me. She says, 'at any time you can pull out ... we won't be mad with you' ... they were really good ... [of procedure] it was a really, really nice place ... it didn't seem like a hospital, that was the best thing about it ... they were friendly, they gave you a hug and when you were walking down they had their arm round you and they were just talking to you about any old thing, trying to take your mind off it.*
(TOP41)

Examples of negative experiences

[NHS contract] *No one would really explain anything, like I didn't know what was happening to me.*
(TOP29)

[NHS] *I didn't like her attitude* [the gynaecologist]. *I asked the nurse afterwards and she said, 'well, you've got to remember she's doing a job but she doesn't necessarily approve of abortions'. That's fair enough, but she's doing a professional job.*
(TOP25)

[NHS] *It was just a job for them I suppose, they get people in and out every day and you're just not very individual.*
(TOP37)

[rated service highly overall, but ...] *... they put me in the children's ward with all the babies round me ... I did find that a bit weird and unfair considering they knew what I was going in for.*
(TOP12)

Normalisation of abortion – where staff were reported to have treated respondents in a caring but friendly manner – emerged frequently in positive accounts. Being given information was also emphasised, because it was experienced as being linked to feeling in control. A further point that was raised related to age. Respondents indicated they had expected to be treated poorly because of their age, but, instead, reported being 'treated like an adult' or being 'not looked down on for being young'.

Accounts of negative experiences highlighted the same points, emphasising lack of information, being treated in a hostile or judgemental manner and age being perceived as an issue. The following extracts illustrate typical accounts of this kind of experience.

These accounts indicate some young women experience choosing abortion as a stigmatising experience, which has particular age-related aspects to it. Services can play an important role in relation to this, in a positive or negative sense. It was notable that there were more negative accounts where respondents accessed NHS-provided consultations and procedures than where they were treated by a specialist provider; this applied in terms of presence or absence of supportiveness, helpfulness and post-abortion care.

As a point of comparison, respondents who continued pregnancies discussed their experience in terms that were as frequently negative as they were positive. Many drew attention to their age being an issue. Just under one-third described their experience in part in negative terms because of the way they perceived a member of staff at the hospital had responded to them because of their age; typical was this comment:

They were alright until I got onto the [labour] *ward. There was one midwife who made it quite clear she didn't agree ... because I was, you know, a teenage mum. She was quite, quite nasty.*
(M37)

Positive accounts also included reference to age, and it was the fact that this did not appear to be an issue for those who cared for the respondents that seemed to make a difference.

Scans
One particular issue that emerged related to scans performed to date pregnancy. Where respondents opted against terminating a pregnancy after having first decided to do so, it was because of this aspect of their experience. This was the case for two respondents, both of whom were strongly encouraged by staff to view the scan images at consultation stage. This experience was viewed negatively, for example:

Interviewer: *What should they have done?*

M5: *Not really said ... [that] the baby is moving round loads or showed you the photos of it.*

One-fifth of those who did proceed to terminate also raised this aspect of their experience as significant; for example:

[NHS] *The scan ... was an emotional point ... I refused to look at the screen ... I told myself, don't look at it, it's not real, and it doesn't matter, you're getting rid of it anyway ... it was actually a maternity ward which is great isn't it!*
(TOP25)

[NHS] *They were alright ... but when I went for the scan the woman ... went, 'oh there's definitely a heartbeat there', and I was like, 'I don't want to know that ... how dare you say that to me'.*
(TOP14)

Some of these respondents had had the abortion many months previously, and practice may have since changed in these units. But their comments do indicate that, where a pregnancy is screened in order to date it, the woman should not be encouraged to view the image unless she says she wants to. Women who are going to have an abortion and those having babies need to be treated differently. Being shown a scan was more common in NHS providers than in non-NHS providers (almost three-quarters of those who mentioned scans in their interviews were treated in NHS hospitals compared with under half of the latter group).

Chapter 3 summary points

1 Over and above the effect of social deprivation, areas with higher abortion proportions tend to have more family planning provision, higher proportions of female GPs and greater independent-sector abortion provision (both NHS and self-funded).

2 GP attitudes and practices do not appear to significantly affect local abortion proportions, with the vast majority reporting that they refer young women for abortion and supporting NHS funding.

3 Waiting times for abortion are generally reported to be in line with government guidelines, although abortion services appear to be struggling to meet targets in some areas.

4 There is a commonly perceived problem in accessing abortion after the first trimester.

5 There are marked local contrasts in attitudes to abortion provision in the NHS. While these do not appear to impact on variations in abortion proportions, they are likely to affect young women's experiences.

6 Generally, young women have made up their mind about whether to end or continue a pregnancy before visiting a doctor.

7 Young women who have positive experiences of abortion care emphasise services being readily available, health professionals respecting their right to choose, providing them with information and being non-judgemental. Those who have a negative experience highlight the same issues and, in addition, report sometimes feeling over-counselled, difficulties in accessing second trimester procedure and their experiences of undergoing dating scans.

8 Most young women who continue pregnancies report positive experiences but a minority feel stigmatised by health professionals because of their age.

4 Interpersonal relationships and abortion decisions

Young women interviewed in Phase Three had mostly become fairly clear in their minds about whether they would end or continue the pregnancy *before* they saw a medical professional. This chapter discusses in more detail the major reported influences over decisions for or against motherhood during this time. It focuses mainly on their interactions with other people who form an important part of the non-clinical context in which pregnancy decisions are made – namely, primarily, partners[1] and parents,[2] but also friends and family friends.

All-age abortion proportions

It is not possible to incorporate these influences in the statistical models developed in this study. However, one aspect that can be explored is whether under-18 abortion proportions are related to the rate or proportion of *all abortions* in a local authority. The assumption here is that, if there is a relationship, it indicates the existence of variations in patterns of reproductive behaviour *generally* that provide the context for decisions *young women* make. Young women in particular localities may have a similar attitude and approach to reproductive choices as older women in their social milieu, for example their mothers, aunties or family friends.

An assessment was made of whether under-18 abortion proportions were related to the rate or proportion of *all* abortions in a local authority in both Phases One and Two. In both phases, the probability of an under-18 abortion increases significantly in line with increases in the all-age abortion proportion, after accounting for deprivation and service provision. In Phase One, this association was found to be lower for under-16s relative to 16–17 year olds, although this was not the case for Phase Two.

There are difficulties involved in interpreting the nature of the statistical relationship between under-18 and all-age abortion proportions. It can be stated, however, that the strength of the all-age abortion proportion factor suggests it represents something more than just deprivation and service provision locally, namely a 'cultural' or 'familial' effect.

Reactions to pregnancy

Before detailing the reported influence of other people, it is important to consider young women's own reported initial reactions to the pregnancy. Perhaps somewhat surprisingly, reactions to the initial *suspicion* of pregnancy did not differ markedly between the two groups; around one-fifth reported reacting with 'shock/horror', fewer than 10 per cent of the maternity group reported feeling 'pleased', around one-fifth of both groups reported 'anxiety' and a quarter of the maternity group reported 'fear of others' reactions'. Both groups reported parents' likely reactions as the major source of their fears, with partners' reactions featuring for one-third.[3]

The time between the initial suspicion of pregnancy (most commonly a missed period) and having a test was either very short (one-quarter reported the same day) or fairly long; one-quarter of the termination group and one-third of the maternity group reported waiting more than four weeks to have a test. Home pregnancy tests were used by almost half of the respondents in both groups, with more of the maternity group visiting a GP surgery.

Confirmation was greeted with high levels of 'shock/horror' by one-third of both groups, followed by 'fear of others' reactions' (high for one-fifth of the termination group and over one-third of the maternity group). Feeling 'pleased' was reported by only 13 per cent of the maternity group and fewer of the termination group. Among those who reacted with reported 'shock/horror', the major reasons among the termination group were 'wrong time to have baby' (80 per cent), 'impact on education/employment' (63 per cent) and 'cannot afford baby' (48 per cent). Among the maternity group, the major reasons were 'wrong time to have baby' (66 per cent), 'impact on education/ employment' (42 per cent) and 'fear of losing partner' (24 per cent).[4]

Both groups were most likely to have first told the partner about the pregnancy, followed by mother and a close friend for the maternity group, and close friend for the termination group. Other people were told by fewer of the termination group, presumably because, in some cases, the termination was carried out without others knowing (in only 60 per cent of cases was the respondent's mother told about the pregnancy). Immediate reactions by partners were reported as being 'very negative' by around one-quarter of respondents in both groups, and 'very pleased' by 10 per cent of the termination group and one-third of the maternity group. Mothers' reactions were reported as being 'very negative' by one-quarter of both groups, although *subsequent* reactions changed quite dramatically; while only 4 per cent of the termination group reported their mothers as being 'very positive' after the initial reaction, almost half of the maternity group did so.

Fourteen per cent of the partners of the termination group were reported as being 'strongly for maternity' compared with 41 per cent of the maternity group's partners. Around one-third of the partners of the termination group were reported as being 'strongly for termination'. In respect of the reactions of mothers, very few of the termination group (among those who knew about the pregnancy) were reported as being in favour of maternity, with the majority being 'somewhat' or 'strongly' in favour of termination. Among the mothers of the maternity group, one-third were

reported as being ambivalent and a further one-third indicated support for termination; only one in seven initially clearly supported maternity as a preferred choice.

Around two-thirds of each group reported that they felt that they had the final choice in the outcome and that their own personal views were very important.

Influence of significant others

The remainder of this chapter discusses the stage of decision making, following the confirmation of the pregnancy, and the ways in which interactions with other people featured in this process. In the analysis of the interviews with young women, 'discussion' of the decision with another person was distinguished from 'influence', and the summary that follows highlights this point. Partners are considered first in regard to their reported degree of influence over abortion and maternity decisions; the same order is then followed with regard to parents. Finally, the reported influence of other people is summarised.

Partners and decision making
Abortion outcomes
A larger proportion of those who terminated than who continued reported they were influenced by their partner (one-half compared to one-quarter). Of those who terminated, in no case was overt violence or coercion involved (in the one case where legal measures were threatened by a partner, it was to prevent an abortion).

In a small number of cases, the influence of the partner was discussed in a way that emphasised the mutuality:

We spoke about it a lot and we both ... thought the same ... I was too young, I wasn't working as such, he was not on enough money.
(TOP3)

More frequently, respondents were ambivalent themselves about what they wanted to do. Had their partner expressed happiness and excitement about the pregnancy, it is possible they would have continued it, but this was not often the case. One such young woman was 15, and explained that she was, in some sense, 'happy to be pregnant', but her boyfriend (of a similar age):

> ... was sort of saying that I had no choice than to have an abortion ... he's like 'you're having a termination' ... so long as he didn't get killed [by his dad] that was fine.
> (TOP44)

Most respondents, and their partners, were older than 15 years and the partner generally made it clear that he was not going to be a father to the child. 'He didn't want it ... we hadn't been together that long', said TOP8. 'He told me to get rid of it ... he already had a child though', explained TOP48. Another said that, '[he] would have left me straight away ... [he] told me, "I will not pay for this child, I do not want this child" ... it got to the extent where it wasn't his baby any more, it was mine' (TOP28).

Three of this group became pregnant again quite quickly after terminating and it was apparent from their narratives that they were strongly driven to have a child. The others, however, explained they were now pleased, looking back on their pregnancy, that they did not continue it; for example 'when I look back on it, it was the right decision' (TOP26).

More than half who terminated described the decision as 'their own' rather than being influenced by their partner, although most of this group did tell them about the pregnancy (consistent with Henderson, 1999). The main theme in their narratives (although not the only one) was aspects of their future life discussed previously, for example:

> I care too much about my education ... at the age of 16 you can't be a mum, that's terrible ... it's the age to have your education.
> (TOP51)

Most who described their decision this way did not perceive their relationship to have longevity. Where they did, women did tell the partners about the pregnancy, but, where the men expressed support for continuation, the women rejected the option:

> I think he was quite looking forward to having it, but I didn't want to ... I just thought, 'well I want to be a teacher so ... have a termination'.
> (TOP32)

> He just says 'what do I want to do?', and I says, 'I wanna get rid of it' and then he goes 'don't you want to keep it?' I said 'it would be nice, but I don't want to'. [She wanted to complete her college course and concentrate on her job.]
> (TOP49)

More did not perceive their relationship with their partner as important or long-term. The pregnancy for a few had resulted from a 'one-night stand' and some did not feel committed to the relationship with the father. Among the former group, one said she made her decision 'instantly', because of university and wanting a career (TOP45). Another was already a mother and reported 'I had the abortion ... just after I'd had my baby ... I'm not having second thoughts, I don't even think about it' (TOP24).

Of this group who did not have relationships that were important to them, telling their partner about the pregnancy often seemed to be a formality:

> I goes 'I'm having a termination, is that alright with you?' He goes 'Yeah that's fine ... it's your decision'. It was my age.
> (TOP2)

TOP12 stated that: 'I didn't see the point in telling him ... But all my friends said ... he had a right to know. In the event, he said the decision was 'up to you'.

Maternity outcomes

The one-quarter of those who continued who reported they were influenced by their partner had quite varied experiences. M12 described her pregnancy as 'planned', but she was in a very violent relationship, and would not have stopped using contraception and had a child were she in a different kind of relationship. This was the only example where there was obvious coercion.

Seven of this group had considered abortion but continued the pregnancy in large part because of opposition to it from their partners. M31 explained that she was not sure it was 'the right time' to have a child, but 'he said, "don't kill my child" ... he wanted it a lot, he didn't want me to kill it'. One got as far as being booked in for an abortion consultation, but when her boyfriend found out:

... he just flipped, 'Oh how could you kill a baby?'... so that made me feel well she's my own ... my daughter inside there, or my baby.
(M52)

In these instances, respondents appeared very concerned to maintain the relationship with their partner, even if doing so involved motherhood at a time that did not seem quite right to them.

In other cases, women emphasised mutuality. They discussed how 'we' made the decision, or the decision was made by 'us'. It was in this respect that the partner was influential:

We knew we were going to try for a baby but we didn't tell anyone ... I think he was really excited but quite worried as well ... it was a bit of an adventure really.
(M17)

Where the decision was reported to be mutual, the partner made it clear he would accept whatever decision the young woman made:

I was in care for a couple of years ... when I met the baby's dad, he sort of straightened me out ... he was totally supportive of whatever I wanted, which is hard in a way because ... if I make this huge decision that's going to affect our lives forever.
(M24)

The majority who continued did not, however, emphasise the influence of their partner.

Partners did not feature at all in seven cases. In two, the child's biological father did not become aware of the pregnancy until after the birth of the child and the others told their partner of the pregnancy at a late gestational stage. In these cases, it seemed respondents did suspect they were pregnant at an earlier stage, but more or less consciously rejected abortion, and did not have the pregnancy confirmed until later. One, who told her partner about the pregnancy at six-and-a-half months, explained, 'I had a feeling and I wasn't bothered ... I knew I wouldn't be able to get rid of him' (M47), and another said, 'I just left it and put it to the back of my head ... I was about seven months when my mum noticed ... then I couldn't get rid of it, but I wouldn't anyway, because I don't believe in abortion' (M42).

The father of the child was mostly reported to have accepted the outcome, even if he was shocked or worried to begin with; he was 'shocked ... but alright as well', 'alright about it', or 'right happy', for example. In most cases, he was reported to have had some relationship with the child following its birth. The pregnancy, however, was very much viewed by the respondent as 'hers', and it was left up to the father to determine whether he wanted to play a role in the upbringing of the child that would result. 'I just wondered if you want 'owt to do with it, if you don't it's fine', was how M51 described her first conversation with the father about the pregnancy; 'he says, "course I want sommat to do with it"', she continued.

Most did tell their partner at an early gestational stage, but it was about the decision that had already been made by them. In other words, while it was considered necessary that the father of the child knew that they were going to have a baby, he was not reported as having been in a position to have influenced the decision. They strongly wanted to have a baby.

A sense of wanting to continue the pregnancy regardless of the existence of a relationship was made very clear in the narratives of those who told their partner, but continued where their partner opposed this outcome:

> He wanted me to get rid of the baby and I ... didn't really want to ... we split up straight away.
> (M1)

> He was just about forcing me [to have an abortion] ... I did think about it but then I thought, well I'm not going to be with him any longer because ... he was messing me about behind my back.
> (M40)

When the partner was, or became, pleased about fatherhood, respondents were very pleased, however:

> He was like, 'oh can I see her on weekends?' ... I didn't think he would react like that.
> (M35)

> [I] felt quite guilty [that she was having the baby] because the relationship was new. I could tell by his face he was worried and scared. [She now lives with him and the child]
> (M16)

Among most of those who continued, therefore, acceptance of the pregnancy by the partner was desired, but it was not the determining factor. It was the respondents' own feelings about the pregnancy – and their wish to continue it – that were presented as stronger and more important than the existence of, and nature of, their relationship.

Parents and decision making
Abortion outcomes
Just less than one-third who terminated did not tell either parent about their pregnancy. Their accounts of non-disclosure emphasised the trepidation and fear experienced by those who continued. Like Harden and Ogden (1999), who found that teenagers who have abortions often experienced unplanned pregnancy as a sign of their 'irresponsibility', these respondents imagined parents would respond badly to the news, and feel ashamed or disappointed, and upset.

Concern about parents finding out about the pregnancy and being angry or disappointed was particularly strong for respondents from religious backgrounds:

'I couldn't have the baby and stay ... because Muslims, you're not allowed to sleep with somebody before you're married and having a baby is way out' (TOP19) – she in fact relied on her uncle throughout for support and practical assistance. Another from a Muslim family was very clear that she wanted to terminate the pregnancy, but could not tell her parents about it: 'they would say, "how did you do this? You shouldn't do this, this is against our culture"' (TOP10). The influence of religious beliefs was also evident in other cases:

> My mum's against abortions because she's Irish and they hate the fact that you are getting rid of a child ... that's why I couldn't tell her.
> (TOP43)

Some from non-religious backgrounds also predicated disapproval from parents; for example, 'I think maybe my family are quite against abortion ... I didn't want anyone else to try and change my mind' (TOP3). Those from non-religious backgrounds tended to emphasise that parents would be upset or disappointed, more than opposition to abortion, however. TOP7 explained, 'If I'd really been thinking about keeping it I would have [told them] ... but I didn't think there was any point ... it would have just worried them'. TOP12 said, 'I think it would have upset my mum … dad would have been really disappointed in me'.

There were also instances where respondents had not told parents, but they found out before the abortion took place. The parent becoming aware of the pregnancy did, in fact, improve the situation; for example:

> I was … only like 16 … obviously you've got the choice of not telling your parents … that was the worst thing about it, the fact that my mum's going to find out … I don't know if you should be encouraged more to tell your parents … at 16, you can't do it on your own really. [Her mother then found out, because she had to stay in overnight for the procedure.] She wasn't upset … well, she was upset with herself I think, because she felt like I couldn't tell her.
> (TOP37)

On some occasions, it was the intervention of a third party that eased the situation; for example:

> [Of a friend's mum] She found me in tears … and just basically said, 'look, it's going to be OK'. That was the first parent words I got, 'it's going to be OK' … she was very supportive, she fulfilled my mum's role, because my mum didn't know at this time.
> (TOP35)

Where respondents did not discuss the pregnancy, the vast majority did gain support and guidance from someone else. This was a partner, another family member, or a person close to the family.

Parents who were told of the pregnancy were described as influential over the decision by young women who had 'mixed feelings' and were looking for guidance about what to do (about one-quarter of the abortion sample). Parents were mostly reported to have responded by presenting their daughter with reasons why it would be better to have an abortion:

> It was like my mum said to me, 'It's up to you but I think at the end of the day it would be best if you had an abortion because you're only 17'. I thought, 'yeah'.
> (TOP4)

> I spoke to my foster mum and she was like, 'you can't have this baby, you know that don't you' … she was, like 'you've got your life sorted, he's going to school next year' [her son] … 'you can get yourself a full-time job, have your own house'.
> (TOP15, had one child already and lives in foster care)

Younger respondents especially found parental guidance of this kind welcome:

> I suppose my mum had a lot of influence … I don't think she wanted me to go through with it because she was scared about my education and my future … and I mean I'm only 15 and I can't make decisions for myself and I need my mum to help me make decisions.
> (TOP44)

In some instances, parents emphasised practical problems associated with their daughter having a baby. TOP2 said she felt 'a bit iffy' about what to do, but her mum, while making it clear she would support her 'either way', said, 'I ain't got any money at the moment' and would not be able to buy things for the baby. TOP28 explained how she was influenced by her mother's experience of being a parent: 'She brought me and my sister up on her own and she said, "it's no life"'. Her mum was more influential then her partner, she continued, 'because I knew I couldn't of really done it without her, so I didn't think it was fair since she'd brought up me and my sister'.

In a few cases, it was the young women's perceptions of their parents' *experience* rather than what the latter said that influenced them. One did not want to 'make the same mistake' as her mum: 'I don't want a kid without a father being there' (TOP14). Another rather vividly explained that 'like Turkish people, before they got a baby when they were 16, 17, and what they did is stay at home, clean, cook … like my mum … I can see she's always at home … I'd prefer dying than living like that' (TOP10).

These examples show that teenage motherhood is not necessarily simply 'passed down' through the generations.

Most who had an abortion, however, described the decision to do so as 'their own'. Around one-quarter of those who terminated pregnancies emphasised this point very strongly indeed, making it very clear that abortion was 'their choice', made independently:

> *When I was late, I told her* [her mum] *... but it was all my decision.*
> (TOP9)

> *It was my decision, it was made in my room, the minute I realised ... I said, 'mum there's something you should know, I'm pregnant ... I've got an appointment at the family planning clinic next Wednesday and it's all going to be sorted out, it's all under control'.*
> (TOP35)

The experience of these young women cannot, however, be understood in separation from parental influence altogether. First, it was notable that some very much sought, or appreciated, parental support and assistance. 'I don't think it was that I was trying to decide because I knew straight away', noted TOP30. But she emphasised how her mum was 'really, really, good about it. She just said "right, OK, don't worry, I'm here for you"'. TOP42 said her parents 'didn't have any influence ... over it'. But she was pleased that her dad said, 'OK we all make mistakes, let's sort it out'. Again, it was younger members of the sample, aged 14 or 15, who were very appreciative of parental support. TOP40 knew what she would do immediately, but emphasised the importance of the moment when she said 'mum, you need to help me'.

Second, most in this group indicated that, while the decision was 'their own', it was one that their parents agreed with:

> *I knew straight away ... I suppose they would have supported me whatever I wanted but I think they probably would have thought it was the right thing for me as well.*
> (TOP33)

> *It was always going to be an abortion ... she said she thought it was the best thing to have a termination ... but, whatever I wanted to do, she'd support me.*
> (TOP47)

> [It was] *very easy, because I didn't want it ... I could tell my mum wanted me to have a termination.*
> (TOP32)

As Chapter 2 discussed, entering higher education figured as an important part of these respondents' perceived future life, as did career and sometimes travel. Parental agreement about abortion being the right choice may reflect shared assumptions about the effect of motherhood for young women in this regard.

Maternity outcomes

A few respondents who continued their pregnancy related attempts by parents to strongly exert their authority to influence the decision:

> *Mum turned round and said 'you're having it aborted', like that it was, as if I didn't have a choice. I said, 'I'm having this baby'. She said, 'Not under my roof, you're not'. I said, 'Well then I'll find somewhere else' ... but it was a different light when she seen it* [on the scan].
> (M38)

It was more likely that, where parents tried to shape the pregnancy outcome and succeeded, they were *opposed* to abortion. Five respondents noted strong parental opposition, three of these continued their pregnancies, in part because of this (the other two terminated without telling their parents):

> *I was kind of hoping for her to say, 'well you're young, get rid of it' ... there was a lot of pressure for me to keep him ... but part of me wanted to anyway.*
> (M31)

About one-third who continued indicated parents had influenced the outcome of the pregnancy in other ways. In these cases (as generally), it was not that respondents reported parents were pleased about the pregnancy. Parents' initial reactions were presented as being angry, upset and worried. However, we found – as did Allen and Bourke-Dowling (1998) – that, following these initial reactions, parents of many who continued were reported to have engaged with the young woman in a 'non-directive' way, posing the outcome of the pregnancy as being 'up to you'.

It is not possible to say how many respondents would have opted for abortion if their parents had not responded this way. As noted already, however, parents of those who terminated were influential where the young woman herself was already 'in two minds' about whether or not she wanted to have a baby. For those who were ambivalent and continued, it was the case that parental 'non-directiveness' made a difference. M1 had arranged an abortion (because her boyfriend was opposed to her continuing the pregnancy) and, when she spoke to her mother, 'she didn't urge me to keep the baby, she didn't urge me to get rid of it, she just said, "whatever you do, I'm there for you" and that was brilliant … that felt like I could do what I needed to do'.

> *I was getting an abortion … I didn't really want to have an abortion … [Mum]* wasn't happy, but she *wasn't angry neither … she said she wouldn't mind, whatever my decision was.*
> (M19)

> *When I found out I was pregnant I didn't want it at first … I was worried … mum said she wasn't bothered as long as it made me happy.*
> (M21)

A few of those who continued reported parents had presented abortion as an option that should be considered:

> *… when I got home there was loads of abortion things on my bed … my dad said he just wanted to give me some options, he wasn't forcing me … I said I didn't want an abortion he supported me.*
> (M14)

But most painted a picture in which they, and their parents, actually disliked abortion. Thus, according to M23, 'My mum will never have an abortion and she hasn't made my mind up for me but she was always that way'. M43 noted that her mum said, 'whatever you decide I'll stick by you', but that, 'she don't agree with them [abortions]'.

Dislike of abortion was also highlighted where some respondents described how a parent had put forward abortion as an 'option'; for example:

> *… at first she says, 'Well it might be better if you get rid of it, you are so young, but whatever you say I'll go along with you' … she would never do it herself [have an abortion] … and she says she knew I could not … she says 'it's not in our nature'.*
> (M51)

It is hard to know the extent to which these accounts of parents' perceived reactions are accurate. However, as discussed previously, many of those who continued indicated they were themselves very keen to do so and reported little conflict with parents after the initial period of shock. This suggests that there are common values and expectations at work, which include a sense that abortion is problematic.

Most who continued (two-thirds) indicated very clearly that they did know themselves what they wanted to do, did not consider abortion at all and were happy to be pregnant once they had got over the shock. In this sense, they did not identify parents as influential over the eventual decision. But they did very much want their parents' support and understanding, and made it clear that they experienced great relief from having told them about the pregnancy and having gained their support:

I was really happy in myself [about being pregnant]
*but I was scared about telling mum ... she didn't
believe me at first ... and then she just said that she
wasn't mad with me ... I said I wanted to keep it.*
(M48)

*She said she wasn't too happy, but she'd stick by me
... I cried and cuddled and it was like, I'm so sorry,
but it's happened now ... once I told my mum I was
happy.*
(M16)

It was often at the point of parental knowledge
of the pregnancy that a sense that respondents were
going to 'have a baby', not just 'be pregnant'
emerged. The pregnancy became increasingly
'public' rather than secret, and parental knowledge
then turned into 'support' – 'support money-wise,
like buying cots and clothes' (M16). Others
emphasised other kinds of support mattered:

*She made it clear she weren't happy but, you know, I
always knew that she was there, and I mean she was
even at his birth.*
(M39)

While this does not pertain directly to decision
making, some respondents' experience had also
been strongly shaped by the fact that their parents
and sometimes grandparents had been prepared to
provide practical support, such as assistance with
parenting, or providing respondents with a place to
live following the birth of their baby. In these
respects, we found, like Tabberer *et al.* (2000), that
teenage motherhood often implies reintegration
into the family, and certainly dependence on the
family, especially following the birth of the child.

Other people

Some respondents referred to others when they
discussed their decision, for example friends, and
they often emphasised the existence of common
views, expectations and experience:

Most of them [her friends] *are against it* [abortion],
just one or two were, you know, 'I'd get rid of it'.
(M6)

I was just telling them [friends] *about it* [the
pregnancy] *and they were really happy.*
(M48)

Additionally, in areas where early motherhood
was relatively commonplace, many respondents
referred to the experience of friends and relatives
who also had a baby young. They highlighted the
normative aspects of early motherhood in their
social milieu:

Most of my friends had babies recently anyway.
(M10)

*She's already got a little boy anyway, he's two in
December ... well when she was pregnant with her
little boy I was pregnant.*
(M40)

Similarly, some who had an abortion indicated
they had common views and experience to their
friends:

*I told one of my closest friends, and she really
thought I was right* [to have an abortion].
(TOP25)

*She would do the same thing, that's why I told her ...
She said 'yeah you are right'.*
(TOP10)

*My mate ... said it would be better getting rid of it
because I'm so young and that.*
(TOP7)

Older relatives also figured in some accounts, as
influential in shaping outcomes:

Nan worked in one [hospital] *and my auntie worked in
one and they'd come home and say all the young girls
were having terminations ... that it's wrong ... there's
people in the world who can't have children and
there's the other people who are killing their children.*
(M22)

At first I just wanted to get rid of the baby ... my sister was like, 'are you sure ...?'. She's had one herself ... there's still a part of her that thinks if I had this one now they'd be this age.
(M32)

Others' negative accounts of the experience of abortion featured as part of this aspect of accounts:

I was going to get rid of it but my auntie told me a horrible story ... my auntie has been through it, and I just couldn't do it anyway.
(M3)

I know people that's had abortions and they say it's really horrible and they'd never do it again.
(M33)

There were some cases where 'second-hand' experience was referred to in less negative terms, however, and additionally young women who terminated a pregnancy indicated they did not consider negative accounts of abortion to be relevant to them:

[Of friend] She says ... she couldn't have an abortion and go through all that ... I think she was trying to say that she couldn't be that sort of person to go through with an abortion.
(TOP14)

[Of her boyfriend's relative] She had one and it affected her quite badly ... she had a termination when she was 15 and I think it really screwed her up so she deliberately got pregnant again.
(TOP47)

These examples show it would be inappropriate to regard young women as simply being 'put off' abortion by others; accounts of others' bad experiences do not provide a *direct* explanation for decisions to continue pregnancies, although they form part of the picture.

Community views

Samples of older people who lived in areas classified as 'socially deprived' were interviewed in Phase Three about their views on and experience of abortion. Most reported similar views to those of the young women interviewed.

When asked about how they would react to the news of a daughter's pregnancy, many reported that they would respect whatever decision the young women made; they would be non-judgemental and leave the choice to her. They would be angry or disappointed at first, but would then offer support. Most also made it pretty clear that they were not really in favour of abortion. A frequent response was along the lines that 'it would be their decision but I would not encourage abortion'. Further, when asked about their views about abortion more generally, a common view – mirroring that found among young women – was that abortion equates with 'murder' or 'killing'. The view that 'the baby has done nothing wrong' and/or 'did not deserve to die' was also mentioned fairly frequently, as was the difficulty they thought 'coping with' the aftermath of an abortion might present.

A further justification for dislike of abortion related to the responsibility of the young parents. In a context where it was felt that sufficient provision was made for contraception availability, then any pregnancy was a mistake and it was felt that 'they should not be able to get away with it'.

Abortion negativity was also expressed where questions were asked about NHS provision. On the one hand, even most of those who expressed personal disagreement with abortions accepted that NHS provision should always be available in some cases; such 'genuine need' always included rape and evidence of physical harm to the foetus, and sometimes included young people by virtue of their age. But it was not the case that abortion was viewed as a necessary and legitimate procedure that should be provided to all who request it.

Rather, common reservations that were expressed referred to a perceived risk of abuse by young people – that abortion may be being used merely as a means of contraception – and it was widely felt that it should not be used just as 'an easy option'. Respondents nearly all agreed with NHS provision, but within limits; exactly where the limit should be drawn varied with some suggesting that one 'mistake' was 'permitted', and others suggesting that 'four or five' should be the cut-off.

Interviews with older people also confirmed the point made above about how the availability of carers in the family home can be an important aspect of the context for some young women's decisions to have children early. Some of those we interviewed – especially those who lived in the most deprived areas – noted that there is a steady supply of grandmothers willing, and in some cases keen, to take on (again) maternal responsibilities. One respondent said:

... it's the grandparents that end up bringing the kids up, I mean I'm not going to name names around on the local estate but just, if you just think, just in these three closes, there's about ten grandkids living with grandparents or grandparent, you know?

Many of these older informants made comment on the 'changing times', with less stigma being associated with early pregnancy and childrearing outside of marriage. Indeed, stigma was considerably more likely to be associated with abortion and they reported there to be little open discussion of the options available to pregnant young women, and secrecy surrounding cases in which a termination was, after all, obtained. There was very strong support among these older respondents for improved education and prevention efforts for young people, and for health professionals to be willing to discuss all available options with them.

Chapter 4 summary points

1 Abortion proportions among under-18s correlate strongly across areas with the probability of abortion proportions among women of all ages.

2 There is no marked difference in young women's reactions to the initial suspicion of pregnancy between those who continued with their pregnancy and those who opted to abort. For all young people, parents' likely reactions are the major source of their fears.

3 Confirmation of pregnancy is greeted with high levels of shock/horror, including by those who continue a pregnancy.

4 Most young women, whether they continue or terminate their pregnancy, describe the decision as 'their own'.

5 Young women who have abortions are more likely to be influenced by their partners. Where pregnancies are continued, young women hope that the partner supports the decision but this is not the determining factor in many cases.

6 Around a third of young women who have abortions do not tell either parent about the pregnancy.

7 Parents of young women who become pregnant are often initially upset and angry.

8 Young women who continue tend to represent parents as 'non-directive' in relation to the pregnancy outcome, whereas those who have abortions are more likely to indicate that parents view abortion as the better outcome.

9 Both young mothers and older people in their communities highlight the importance of family support with childcare and parenting.

10 Young women who continue pregnancies often report that having babies young is not unusual in their social circle. Those who have abortions tend to report their friends would do likewise.

5 Summary and conclusions

This research project combined high-level statistical analyses of complex datasets, alongside readings of some detailed and highly personal accounts. Neither of these approaches, nor the various surveys also conducted, provided clear-cut answers to the initial research questions. However, some very clear patterns emerged – some replicating earlier work and some new – that help in our understanding of why variation exists in pregnancy outcomes among teenagers.

An important finding is that, in general, decisions regarding whether to terminate or to continue a pregnancy are made by young women after discovering they are pregnant (as both groups had similar views of their pregnancy) and before visiting a health professional. Thus the variation in abortion proportions is generally determined during this time. Decision making appears to be influenced by their socio-economic circumstances, family and community views, and availability of services. The primary factor accounting for the variation is social deprivation, followed by interpersonal factors, then service provision; this is the order in which the key issues are discussed below.

Social deprivation

More deprived areas have higher conception rates and a lower proportion of under-18 pregnancies ending in abortion. Examination of data at a smaller level of aggregation confirms the association identified at the local authority level. The importance of social deprivation also appears to be greater for determining abortion proportions for 16–17 year olds than it does for those aged under 16 years at conception.

The question raised by these results concerns the extent to which the association with social deprivation can be viewed as causation – that is to say, what is the relationship between social deprivation and abortion proportions? Social deprivation, as a category, explains nothing directly, but the qualitative data have generated some insights concerning how young women living in different communities think about abortion and motherhood.

In the event of experiencing an unplanned pregnancy, those young women whose background and experience mean they have a strong belief that their future life will and should centrally include activities that are 'not motherhood yet' (most importantly, higher education and career development) are clear and decisive in their choice of abortion. By contrast, many of those who continue their pregnancies have a life experience that means motherhood can be perceived in a relatively more positive light, since it does not appear to interfere with plans for the immediate future. On the contrary, it can appear to provide direction in life, the opportunity to take personal responsibility and, in some cases, a close personal relationship with a valued other. Some young women from deprived backgrounds therefore find the prospect of motherhood attractive, to some degree at least. Such young women do often strongly eschew abortion, but this is not simply because of an abstract belief in the idea that abortion is always 'wrong', but rather because their negative view of abortion is formed by the way pregnancy and motherhood appears to them.

Most of the mothers interviewed for this study did not clearly associate motherhood with lack or loss. While there was an association made between motherhood and 'missing out', this was compensated by feelings of excitement about pregnancy and a view of motherhood, once experienced, by some as in many ways rewarding, associated with responsibility and sometimes a spur to achievement. This aspect of young women's experience does not detract in any sense from the problem of social deprivation.

Interpersonal relationships and attitudes to pregnancy and abortion

Statistically significant unexplained variation in abortion proportions remains once social deprivation has been accounted for. A very interesting statistical finding is that, after accounting for deprivation and abortion services, there is a correlation between abortion proportions for all women and those for under-18s. This correlation at least indicates that similar processes are shaping the reproductive behaviour of different age groups. That this association remains after controlling for service provision indicates that familial or community cultures have an impact.

The qualitative work considered this aspect of variation in abortion proportions further, in so far as family and community attitudes towards abortion, pregnancy and motherhood were explored. The findings reported here about this issue are tentative, in particular because they rely strongly on young women's reports of others' attitudes. However, young women's reports of others' attitudes and responses to the formers' pregnancies were revealing.

Few respondents reported that they had actually thought in great detail about the issues involved prior to the event. Some had clear prior views for or against abortion (even though, when faced with the situation, they may not have shown consistency), but many thought about it for the first time only when faced with a crisis in their lives. Even those with clear views were frequently at a loss to describe from where they had originated.

Discussion with respondents highlighted that, when a pregnancy does occur, many young women perceive the outcome to be *their* decision. Many young women who continued could countenance motherhood outside the context of a clearly stable relationship with the father of the child-to-be, although male involvement was viewed as desirable. (It was notable that many of those who terminated pregnancies with 'mixed feelings' about

doing so felt more strongly that they could continue only in the context of greater relationship stability.) Decisions to terminate were also often viewed as their choice, indicating that, overall, young women do view pregnancy decisions as first and foremost theirs to make.

Young women's perceptions of the place of motherhood in their future lives appear to be shaped, even if this is not experienced as a direct process, by community and family views and experience, however. These include the extent to which having children relatively early is accepted and normalised, the importance placed on life goals that are not compatible with early motherhood, and through differing perceptions of the difficulties and demands that parenthood carries with it. The value of the availability of local (and often free) practical assistance should not be underestimated.

Those who aborted tended to indicate that their parents viewed abortion in a pragmatic way and viewed continued pregnancy for young women, and certainly for their daughter, to be a more negative outcome than abortion. By contrast, 'abortion negativity' was more likely to be reported among the parents of those who continued their pregnancy. Interviews with older parents living in socially deprived areas indicated that abortion was viewed fairly negatively. These interviews also drew attention to the way that family members – especially female family members – play a very important role where young women proceed with pregnancies, in that they sometimes step in and take on much of the responsibility for childrearing.

Where others in local communities – friends or neighbours, for example – were the focus of discussion, here, too, attention was drawn to common attitudes and common views about abortion. Hence, young women who readily chose abortion indicated that their friends would do the same, while those who continued their pregnancies and who viewed abortion as 'wrong' highlighted how relatives and neighbours thought the same, as well as reporting that they knew other young women who had also had babies at a young age.

The effects of social deprivation and interpersonal relationships mean that many young women – in the case of this study, just a majority – decide what to do about an unplanned pregnancy in a way that is relatively dilemma-free (in the sense they have strong feelings themselves about what the outcome of the pregnancy should be). A large minority, however, are fairly ambivalent and find making a decision more difficult.

Those in this category who opt for abortion view it as the 'right thing to do' and the 'responsible choice', and they explain the reasoning behind their decision in various ways, particularly through reference to their future plans, their lack of financial independence and the absence of stable relationships that might surround them as a mother. For this group of young women, 'abortion negativity' makes considering (and sometimes then choosing) abortion difficult. Further, evidence shows that almost all young women who choose abortion – even where they are immediately very sure it is the right choice – find it stigmatising. For example, it is viewed as an experience that should be kept secret from parents, and young women who have an abortion are pleasantly surprised when they find health professionals who treat them with sympathy and without judgement.

Abortion services

Decisions about whether to end or continue a pregnancy were rarely influenced directly by a clinician. Most, whether they ended or continued pregnancies, had come to a pretty clear decision about what they wanted to do before they booked an appointment with a referring doctor.

However, statistical analyses did indicate that abortion proportions are related to service provision, after controlling for deprivation, in three ways. These are family planning clinic provision, the proportion of female GPs and how abortion

services are provided – specifically, the availability of independent-sector provision. Caution is needed in regard to the last two of these. It may be that independent-sector clinics have been sited in areas with higher abortion proportions, and cultural and/or socio-economic factors may have an independent association with the probability of female GPs.

In relation to family planning provision, it appears that young women are more likely to regard this type of service as a place to go for abortion referral, as opposed to GP services, possibly for reasons of anonymity or because of perceptions of service relevance. Thus, a lack of family planning provision may restrict choices regarding outcomes of pregnancies and thus lead to lower abortion proportions.

The qualitative research highlighted some other important general aspects of abortion services. NHS-funded abortion services are almost always available where young women request abortion; however, other problems pertain. In some instances, local services are struggling to meet demand and, in a small number of cases, waiting times are longer than they should be. Further, abortion after the first trimester appears to be disliked by many clinicians and difficult to access. In regard to quality of care, care from the independent providers was experienced more positively than that from the NHS.

Problems in referral, created by strong moral opposition to abortion being encountered by young women, did not emerge as a clear barrier to access to abortion. Making their disapproval of teenage pregnancy and/or abortion apparent, trying to shift young women towards another professional as fast as possible and being unhelpful in regard to access to abortion after the first trimester were all problematic and upsetting features of the referral process for some young women, however. These are important issues, since young women feeling anxious about seeking abortion, and often being unclear about what to do and what will happen, perceive it to be very important that referring doctors make it clear that they will assist them in obtaining whichever services they need and will fully explain the process. Particularly for those seeking abortion, it was important that referring doctors gave reassurance that it would be possible to access the procedure and that they would do all they could to make sure this happened in a speedy fashion.

Policy implications

This report began by referring to fertility pathways involving a series of 'choices'; it concludes by acknowledging that, while the term 'choice' is an appropriate one to use, there are many disparate elements that contribute to the final outcome for individuals. Young women's decisions about pregnancy are shaped by social deprivation, mediated through interpersonal relationships. Abortion remains stigmatised; there are also disparities in access to abortion services and services vary in quality. In this light, policy should take into account the following.

- It is necessary to accept and build on the satisfaction many young women get from motherhood and they need medical services that accept their choice. Other initiatives should aim to raise expectations in regard to what can be achieved through education and through success in the world of work.

- Abortion needs to be destigmatised. It would be advantageous for the case to be made more strongly in public arenas by those with influence over policy making that abortion is accepted as an aspect of reproductive health care and family planning, and that it is morally acceptable for women to choose to abort pregnancies. Greater discussion in school-based sex and relationships education, or the wider availability of literature that spells out the options, would also be ways of achieving this.

- There are some aspects of service provision that directly impact on abortion proportions and these should be addressed. They include access to family planning and sexual health services, better access to abortion through existing GP services, the availability of local NHS provision and independent-sector abortion provision.

- Abortion services should not vary in quality in the way they do currently. Referrers need to support and assist young women seeking abortion. There is a range of issues, other than waiting times, that abortion services need to improve on. These include access to second trimester procedures, and sympathetic and caring treatment at consultation and procedure, which takes fully into account the needs of young women undergoing abortion.

Notes

Chapter 1

1. Such as Standardised Mortality Ratios for regional health authorities (RHAs) and the Jarman Deprivation Index.

2. This particular study used the Carstairs Index of Deprivation.

3. All aspects of the research were approved by the North West MREC (reference numbers 01/8/7, 01/8/72 and 02/8/54).

4. The Technical Report is available from the Centre for Sexual Health Research, University of Southampton.

5. This refers to local authority districts within counties.

6. A specific problem was the different collation of routine conception data in Scotland, where under-18 data are not routinely produced. Unlike England and Wales, Scottish conception data include miscarriages and the date of conception is taken from the date of conception outcome rather than backdating to an estimated date of conception. These two factors were specifically altered in the data provided for Scotland, so that they would be comparable to data collated by the Office for National Statistics. However, as the Scottish conception data are collated from hospital records data, and not birth registration and abortion notification records (as for England and Wales), the two sets of data are not identical.

7. A method for analysing the extent to which each of a range of different potential explanatory variables are independently associated with an event that has one of two possible outcomes (in this case maternity or abortion).

8. The sites were: low conception and low abortion proportion (AP): Isle of Wight and Norfolk; low conception and medium AP: Trafford and Cambridgeshire; low conception and high AP: Richmond and North Somerset; medium conception and low AP: Leeds and Northumberland; medium conception and medium AP: Vale of Glamorgan and Lincolnshire; medium conception and high AP: Wirral and Enfield; high conception and low AP: Telford and Wrekin and Bridgend; high conception and medium AP: Greenwich and Swindon UA; high conception and high AP: Islington and Lambeth. The Scottish sites were Ayrshire and Arran (low AP), Greater Glasgow (medium AP) and Lothian (high AP).

Chapter 2

1. Under-16 conceptions are included in the numbers but the population base refers to 15–17 year olds.

2. These are listed in Appendix 1.

3. Quintiles represent roughly one-fifth of the national distribution.

4. The ONS area classification groups together local authorities that have similar socio-economic and demographic profiles across a broad range of measures (Bailey *et al.*, 2000). The names such as 'Inner London' are chosen to reflect the socio-economic profile and general location of authorities in this group.

5. For example, 50 per cent of local authorities have less than or equal to 0.4 per cent African-Caribbean population of females aged 13–17.

6   Twenty-two standardised deprivation measures derived from the Carstairs, Department of Environment, Jarman and Townsend indices; the full list is shown in Appendix 2.

7   This is a common indicator of a group 'at risk' from deprivation, but it could also be representative of the local culture towards childbearing.

Chapter 3

1   Map 3 shows the percentages of abortions funded and performed by the NHS in each local area. Additionally, the locations of bpas centres that perform NHS agency abortions are indicated.

2   A list is provided in Appendix 2.

3   Where there was no GP surgery in the ward, the women were considered to have no local provision.

4   These were formulated by Lords Fraser and Scarman as the House of Lords response to the case of Victoria Gillick versus East Norwich and Wisbech HA and the DHSS. They stipulate the conditions under which a doctor or other health professional can provide contraceptives to a woman under the age of 16 years without parental consent.

5   The dimensions were: the ability of the units *in the site* to meet local demand for the service, the availability of first trimester procedures, the availability of procedures performed later in gestation, the referral process, as a whole, for under-18s (routes of access measure), the access to NHS-funded procedures, the specific measures available for under-18s who terminate pregnancies and the accessibility of TOP for under-18s overall.

6   Questionnaire studies were carried out among NHS staff only.

7   Individual attribution of comments has been withheld for reasons of confidentiality.

Chapter 4

1   By this term, we refer to the male, irrespective of relationship status, by whom the respondent became pregnant.

2   By this term, we include carers and guardians, as well as biological and step-parents.

3   Although percentage figures are shown in this chapter, because of the small samples, these should not be taken too literally; they are used to give a rough guide to the comparisons being presented. Equally, the samples cannot be regarded as being representative of all young women who conceive.

4   Multiple codings were possible for the analysis of this item, so percentages add to more than 100.

References

Abortion Law Reform Association (ALRA) (1997) *A Report on NHS Abortion Services*. London: ALRA

Abortion Law Reform Association (ALRA) (1999) *Improving Access to Abortion, A Guide*. London: ALRA

Allen, I. (1985) *Counselling Services for Sterilisation, Vasectomy and Termination of Pregnancy*. London: Policy Studies Institute

Allen, I. (1990) *Family Planning and Pregnancy Counselling Services for Young People under 25*. London: Policy Studies Institute

Allen, I. and Bourke-Dowling, S. (with Heather Rolfe) (1998) *Teenage Mothers, Decisions and Outcomes*. London: Policy Studies Institute

Bailey, S., Charlton, J., Dollamore, G. and Fitzpatrick, J. (2000) 'Families, groups and clusters of local and health authorities: revised for authorities in 1999', *Population Trends*, Vol. 99, pp. 37–52

Boyle, M. (1997) *Re-thinking Abortion*. London: Routledge

British Pregnancy Advisory Service (bpas) (1978) *Schoolgirl Pregnancies*. Austy Manor: bpas

Burghes, L. (with Mark Brown) (1995) *Single Lone Mothers: Problems, Prospects and Policies*. London: Family Policy Studies Centre

Clements, S. (2002) 'A study of the geographic variation in teenage conceptions and teenage conception outcomes in Great Britain', PhD thesis, University of Southampton

(The) Countryside Agency (2000) *The State of the Countryside 2000*. Cheltenham: Countryside Agency Publications

Department of Health (2001) *The National Strategy for Sexual Health and HIV*. London: Department of Health

Department of Health (2003) *Abortion Statistics, England and Wales, 2002*. London: HMSO

Diamond, I., Clements, S., Stone, N. and Ingham, R. (1999) 'Spatial variation in teenage conceptions in south and west England', *Journal of the Royal Statistical Society* A, Vol. 162, No. 3, pp. 271–89

Furedi, A. (1998) 'Wrong but the right thing to do: public opinion and abortion', in E. Lee (ed.) *Abortion Law and Politics Today*. Basingstoke: Macmillan Press

Garlick, R., Ineichen, B. and Hudson, F. (1993) 'The UPA score and teenage pregnancy', *Public Health*, Vol. 107, pp. 135–9

Harden, A. and Ogden, J. (1999) 'Young women's experiences of arranging and having abortions', *Sociology of Health and Illness*, Vol. 21, No. 4, pp. 426–44

Henderson, L.R. (1999) 'A survey of teenage pregnant women and their male partners in the Grampian region', *British Journal of Family Planning*, Vol. 25, No. 3, pp. 90–2

Hoffman, Saul D. (1998) 'Teenage childbearing is not so bad after all ... or is it? A review of the new literature', *Family Planning Perspectives*, Vol. 30, No. 5, pp. 236–9, 243

Jewell, D., Tacchi, J. and Donovan, J. (2000) 'Teenage pregnancy: whose problem is it?', *Family Practice*, Vol. 17, No. 6, pp. 522–8

Kumar, U., Baraitser, P., Morton, S. and Massil, H. (2004) 'Decision making and referral prior to abortion: a qualitative study of women's experiences', *Journal of Family Planning and Reproductive Health Care*, Vol. 30, No. 1, pp. 51–4

Lane Committee (1974) *Report of the Committee on the Working of the Abortion Act*. London: HMSO

Lo, S.V., Kaul, S., Kaul, R., Cooling, S. and Calvert, J.P. (1994) 'Teenage pregnancy – contraceptive use and non-use', *British Journal of Family Planning*, Vol. 20, pp. 79–83

Luker, K. (1996) *Dubious Conceptions, the Politics of Teenage Pregnancy*. Cambridge, MA: Harvard University Press

Macintyre, S. and Cunningham-Burley, S. (1993) 'Teenage pregnancy as a social problem: a perspective from the United Kingdom', in A. Lawson and D. Rhodes (eds) *The Politics of Pregnancy, Adolescent Sexuality and Public Policy*. New Haven, CT: Yale University Press

McLeod, A. (2001) 'Changing patterns of teenage pregnancy: population based study of small areas', *British Medical Journal*, Vol. 323, pp. 199–203

Marie Stopes International (1999) *General Practitioners: Attitudes to Abortion*. London: Marie Stopes International

Moore, S. and Rosenthal, D. (1993) *Sexuality in Adolescence*. London: Routledge

National Research Council (1987) *Risking the Future, Adolescent Sexuality, Pregnancy, and Childbearing*. Washington DC: National Academy Press

Ooms, T. (ed.) (1981) *Teenage Pregnancy in a Family Context*. Philadelphia, PA: Temple University Press

Pearson, V., Owen, M., Phillips, D., Pereira Gray, D. and Marshall, M. (1995) 'Teenage pregnancy: a comparative study of teenagers choosing termination of pregnancy or antenatal care', *Journal of the Royal Society of Medicine*, Vol. 88, No. 7, pp. 384–8

Phoenix, A. (1991) *Young Mothers?* Cambridge: Polity Press

Plotnick, R.D. (1993) 'The effect of social policies on teenage pregnancy and childbearing', *Families in Society: The Journal of Contemporary Human Services*, Vol. 74, June, pp. 324–8

Pope, M., Adler, N.E., Tschann, J.M. (2001) 'Postabortion psychological adjustment: are minors at increased risk?', *Journal of Adolescent Health*, Vol. 29, No. 1, pp. 2–11

Royal College of Obstetricians and Gynaecologists (RCOG) (1991) *Report of the RCOG Working Party on Unplanned Pregnancy*. London: RCOG

Royal College of Obstetricians and Gynaecologists (RCOG) (2000) *The Care of Women Requesting Induced Abortion*. London: RCOG Press

Seamark, C.J. and Pereira Gray, D.J. (1996) 'Do teenagers consult general practitioners for contraceptive advice?', *British Journal of Family Planning*, Vol. 21, pp. 50–1

Sheldon, S. (1997) *Beyond Control, Medical Power and Abortion Law*. London: Pluto Press

Smith T. (1993) 'Influence of socioeconomic factors on attaining targets for reducing teenage pregnancies', *British Medical Journal*, Vol. 306, pp. 1232–5

Social Exclusion Unit (1999) *Teenage Pregnancy*. London: The Stationery Office

(The) Stationery Office (TSO) (2003) *Government Response to the Health Select Committee's Third Report of Session 2002–03 on Sexual Health*. Cm. 5959. London: TSO

Tabberer, S., Hall., C., Prendergast, S. and Webster, A. (2000) *Teenage Pregnancy and Choice, Abortion or Motherhood: Influences on the Decision*. York: Joseph Rowntree Foundation

Wallace, M., Charlton, J. and Denham, C. (1995) 'The new OPCS area classifications', *Population Trends*, Vol. 79, pp. 15–30

Wellings, K. and Kane R. (1999) 'Trends in teenage pregnancy in England and Wales: how can we explain them?', *Journal of the Royal Society of Medicine*, Vol. 92, June, pp. 277–82

Welsh, P., McCarthy M. and Cromer B. (2001) 'Abortion in adolescence: a four country comparison', *Women's Health Issues*, Vol. 11, No. 2, pp. 73–9

Whitehead, E. (2001) 'Teenage pregnancy: on the road to social death', *International Journal of Nursing Studies*, Vol. 38, No. 4, pp. 437–46

Wilson, S.H., Brown, T.P. and Richards, R.G. (1992) 'Teenage conceptions and contraception in the English regions', *Journal of Public Health Medicine*, Vol. 14, No. 1, pp. 17–25

Appendix 1

Phase One analysis

Table A1.1 Sources of data collected for Phase One

Data	Source
Abortion/fertility measures	
Percentage of under 16/16–17/under 18/all-age conceptions that were aborted	ONS/ISD
Under 16/16–17/under 18 conception rates	ONS/ISD
Under-18/all-age abortion rate 1997–99	Department of Health/ISD
Availability of abortion	
Provision of bpas clinics and consultation centres as of 1999	bpas
Provision of Marie Stopes clinics and consultation centres as of 1999	Marie Stopes
Provision of Brook Advisory Centres as of 1999	Brook
Funding of under-18 abortions (NHS/NHS Agency/Non-NHS)**	ONS
Funding of all-age abortions (NHS/NHS Agency/Non-NHS)**	Department of Health
Demographic/socio-economic factors	
ONS area classification	ONS (2000) Families, Groups and Clusters of Local and Health Authorities: Revised for Authorities in 1999. Population Trends 99, pp. 37–52
Percentage of females aged 18–24 who were unemployed in mid-1998	ONS – NOMIS database; population estimates: ONS/GRO
Percentage of 15/16 year olds obtaining five or more GCSEs in 1998	England: DfEE (1999) *GCSE/GNVQ and GCE A/AS/Advance GNVQ Results for Young People in England, 1998/99*, Table 13; Scotland: ONS (2000) *Regional Trends 35*, Table 16.3; Wales: ONS (1999) *Examination Achievements: Gender Analysis*. Statistical brief SDB 60/99, Table 1
Percentage of looked-after children aged 0–17 in 1998	England: DoH (1999) – *Children Looked After by LAs Year ending 31st March 1999, England*, Table 3; Scotland: Scottish Executive Education Department – *Information on Looked After Children: at 31st March 1997 and 1998*, Annex 1; Wales: Statistics Wales (1999) *Social Services Report*, Table 1.6; Population estimates: ONS/GRO
Percentage of 11–15 year olds who were dependants of income support claimants as of August 1998	ONS – Neighbourhood Statistics; population estimates: ONS/GRO
Percentage of 11–15 year olds who were dependants of family credit claimants as of August 1999	ONS – Neighbourhood Statistics; population estimates: ONS/GRO
Index of Multiple Deprivation 2000, average of ward scores*	ONS – Neighbourhood Statistics
Carstairs Index	Derived from 1991 census small area statistics
Percentage of 16/17 year olds participating in education in 1997–98*	DfEE (1999) *Statistics of Education: Participation in Education and Training by Young People Aged 16 and 17 in Each Local Area and Region, England, 1993/94 to 1997/98*
Percentage of females aged 13–17 by ethnic group (as of mid-1998)	Centre for Census and Survey Research, University of Manchester

GRO (General Register Office for Scotland); ISD (Information and Statistics Division of the Scottish Health Service); ONS (Office for National Statistics)
*Data collected only for England; **Data collected only for England and Wales

Table A1.2   Phase One models

Factor	Model 1	Model 2	Model 3	Model 4	Model 5
Age					
Under 16	1.67***	1.67***	1.67***	1.67***	1.67***
16–17 (Ref.)	1.00	1.00	1.00	1.00	1.00
ONS area classification					
Mining, Manufacturing and Industry (Ref.)		1.00	1.00	1.00	1.00
Coast and Services		1.28***	1.19***	1.18***	1.16***
Urban Fringe		1.49***	1.19***	1.18***	1.20***
Rural Areas		1.67***	1.36***	1.39***	1.51***
Prosperous England		2.03***	1.37***	1.36***	1.50***
Education Centres and Outer London		2.12***	1.49***	1.46***	1.04
Inner London		2.43***	1.83***	1.76***	0.93
Dependants of family credit claimants (%)			0.96***	0.97***	0.97***
Under-18 abortions performed by the NHS (%)				0.999***	1.00
bpas provision					
Abortion centre				1.23**	1.12
Consultation centre only				0.95	0.88**
No centre (Ref.)				1.00	1.00
Conceptions aborted by all women (%)					1.04***
Local authority variance	0.128***	0.055***	0.042***	0.038***	0.029***

Figures presented are odds ratios from multilevel logistic regression analysis (except for LA variance); Ref. = Reference category; ***$p<0.001$; **$p<0.01$

Notes:

The odds of an abortion decreases by 0.1 per cent for every 1 per cent increase in the NHS funding and provision of under-18 abortions. While this may appear to be a small change, it is nonetheless highly significant. This is because NHS provision can range widely from 0 to 100 per cent between local authorities. Therefore, an authority that funds and performs all under-18 abortions for its residents will have 10 per cent lower odds of an abortion compared to an authority that funds and performs no under-18 abortions.

The all-age abortion proportion has had a significant effect on the ONS classification. There is now no difference in the chance of an abortion between the two *London* areas and *Mining, Manufacturing and Industry* areas. However, in *Prosperous* and *Rural* areas, the odds of an abortion remain significantly higher and the association with the dependants of family credit claimants remains the same. This suggests that there is little relationship between deprivation and the all-age abortion proportion. Indeed, the correlation between the dependants of family credit claimants and the all-age abortion proportion is –0.11 compared to –0.68 for under-18 abortion proportions.

The all-age abortion proportion has also reduced the importance of the service-related factors. This indicates that they too are associated with, and may well predict, the all-age abortion proportion. However, in Chapter 3, it was noted that the all-age abortion proportions may influence bpas provision as well as vice versa. It is also possible that the funding of under-18 abortions is partly determined by the all-age abortion proportion. Thus, it is likely that the associations here are operating in both directions.

Appendix 2

Further details of Phase Two analysis

Table A2.1 Additional data collected for Phase Two

Data	Source
Availability of abortion	
Facilities providing abortion in 1998 and number of abortions provided to all women by gestation and procedure (LA)	Department of Health/ISD
Ratio of abortions provided in early gestation for teenagers relative to women aged 25–29 in 1997–99 (LA)	Department of Health/ISD
Routes of access	
Location of GP surgeries and characteristics of GPs (aged under 40/gender/provision of contraception to all patients) (1999 – England) (W/LA)	Primary Health Care Database for England NHS for Scotland
Location of GP surgeries and characteristics of GPs (age/gender/registered to provide contraception) (2002 – Scotland) (W/LA) Age and gender of GPs (1999 – Wales) (LA)	Department of Health: General and Personal Medical Services Statistics (Wales)
Location and characteristics (number of days open per week/number of youth days open per week/ NHS abortion referral) of family planning clinics 2002* (LA)	FPA/Sexwise online databases
Demographic/socio-economic factors	
Percentage of females aged 13–17 by ethnic group (as of mid-1998) (W)	Centre for Census and Survey Research, University of Manchester
Standardised deprivation components of the Carstairs, Department of Environment, Jarman and Townsend indices (W)	Calculated using 1991 Census data
ONS classification (W)	Wallace *et al.* (1995)
Proportion of boarding school pupils (W)	Calculated using 1991 census data
Dependants aged 11–15 of income support claimants, August 1998 (%) (W)	ONS – Neighbourhood Statistics Population estimates: Centre for Census and Survey Research, University of Manchester
Dependants aged 11–15 of family credit claimants, August 1999 (%) (W)	ONS – Neighbourhood Statistics Population estimates: Centre for Census and Survey Research, University of Manchester
Percentage of 16- to 19-year-old females married or living as a couple (LA)	ONS/GRO – census 2001

GRO (General Registrar Office for Scotland); ISD (Information and Statistics Division of the Scottish Health Service); ONS (Office for National Statistics). LA = Local authority measure; W = Ward measure
* Brook services are included only for those present as of 1999; thus Brook in Trafford is excluded from the dataset

Table A2.2 Phase Two model results

Factor	Model 1	Model 2	Model 3	Model 4	Model 5
Age					
16–17 (Ref.)	1.00	1.00	1.00	1.00	1.00
Under 16	1.60***	1.60***	1.60***	1.60***	1.60***
Urban (Ref.)		1.00	1.00	1.00	1.00
Rural-Fringe		1.78***	1.09	1.07	1.06
Rural		1.71***	1.13	1.14	1.12
Unemployment			0.74***	0.72***	0.69***
17 year olds not in FTE			0.83***	0.83***	0.86***
Dependants of FCC			0.82***	0.82***	0.83***
Under-fives			0.91***	0.91***	0.90***
5+ GCSEs (LA)				0.98**	0.99
African-Caribbean (%)					1.02***
LA variance	0.133***	0.132***	0.074***	0.060***	0.045***
Ward variance	0.271***	0.240***	0.060***	0.059***	0.054***

Figures presented are odds ratios from multilevel logistic regression analysis; ***$p<0.001$; **$p<0.01$; LA = local authority; FTE = full-time education; FCC = family credit claimants

Notes:

The findings indicate that a 1 per cent increase in those obtaining five or more GCSEs is associated with a 2 per cent lower odds of an abortion. The main reason for this association is, first, that some London sites (for example, Lambeth) have high abortion proportions but much lower GCSE pass rates. Second, the indicator is measured at the site level and so, unlike the ward deprivation indicators, it is not picking up variation in GCSE passes within sites that may be showing a positive association with abortion proportions.

However, this factor becomes non-significant once African-Caribbeans are accounted for. This is because areas with African-Caribbeans tend to have fewer GCSE passes. This does not necessary imply a direct relationship between these two measures.

Table A2.3   Phase 2 model results (continued)

Factor	Model 6	Model 7	Model 8	Model 9
Age				
16–17	1.00	1.00	1.00	1.00
Under 16	1.60***	1.60***	1.60***	1.60***
Urban	1.00	1.00	1.00	1.00
Rural-Fringe	1.08	1.12	1.12	1.11
Rural	1.15	1.20	1.21	1.18
Unemployment	0.69***	0.67***	0.68***	0.68***
17 year olds not in FTE	0.86***	0.86***	0.86***	0.86***
Dependants of FCC	0.84***	0.86***	0.86***	0.85***
Under-fives	0.89***	0.90***	0.90***	0.90***
African-Caribbeans (%)	1.02***	1.01**	1.01*	1.01*
All abortions in LA funded by non-NHS				
0–24%	1.00	1.00	–	–
25%+	1.35**	1.12	–	–
Female GPs (LA%)		1.01*	1.01	–
FP Days Open Index		1.06**	1.03	–
All-age abortions (%)		–	1.02*	1.03***
Local authority variance	0.045***	0.031**	0.025**	0.025**
Ward variance	0.054***	0.054***	0.055***	0.055***

Figures presented are odds ratios from multilevel logistic regression analysis; ***$p<0.001$; **$p<0.01$; *$p<0.05$; LA = local authority; FTE = full-time education; FCC = family credit claimants

Notes:

In Phase Two, the all-age abortion proportion is also highly significant (Models 8 and 9). However, the referral service indicators become non-significant. This indicates that the referral services also influence the all-age abortion proportions, as these factors must therefore be associated and it is hard to justify that the referral service provision is likely to be determined by higher abortion proportions. This is particularly the case for family planning provision, which is likely to be greater where conception rates are higher and thus abortion proportions are lower. However, it is possible that cultural factors influencing the abortion proportions may be similar to those influencing the presence of female GPs. Overall, the strength of the all-age abortion proportion factor suggests that it is accounting for more than just referral service provision.

Survey of teenage pregnancy co-ordinators

In order to gain an overview of provision in the 21 sites at the outset of Phase Two, a questionnaire was mailed to the relevant teenage pregnancy co-ordinators. The topics covered are shown in the box below; a 100 per cent return rate was achieved.

Topics covered on questionnaire for *teenage pregnancy co-ordinators* **in Phase Two sites (most items used five-point rating scales with space for additional comments)**

- Requested list of abortion providers in local authority area.
- Views on sufficiency to meet demand.
- Ease with which women aged under 18 years get NHS procedures.
- Perceived reasons for some young women opting to use private facilities.
- What they know about the views of local consultants.
- Existence of any particularly influential people in local area.
- Available routes of referral locally.
- Perceptions of proportion of GPs who will sign HSA1 and their practice if they do not.
- Whether local young people's sexual health services provide information and refer for abortion.
- Specific initiatives to signpost abortion services.
- Local presence of active anti-abortion groups.
- Perceptions of reasons in local authority for local variations in abortion proportions.

Survey of local abortion commissioners

Similarly, a questionnaire was posted to the abortion service commissioners in each site; a 100 per cent return rate was achieved. The topics covered are shown in the box below.

Topics covered on questionnaire for *commissioners* **in Phase Two sites during (a) the period 1997– 99 and (b) the present time**

- Budget under which abortion is/was provided.
- Contracts with whom for abortion provision.
- Contracts with whom for pregnancy counselling.
- Presence of a service specification and restrictions on eligibility for NHS-funded treatment.
- Existence of case-flow restrictions.
- Available route of access.
- Targets for maximum waiting times.
- Availability of abortion at all gestations.
- Adequacy of abortion provision.
- Groups or individuals with influence over the shape and extent of abortion services.
- Changes to policy and practice following publication of national strategies.

Survey of hospital consultants

Finally, a questionnaire was mailed to all consultants working in departments of obstetrics and gynaecology in the hospitals in the 21 sites; 190 questionnaires were returned. The topics covered are shown below.

Topics covered on questionnaire for *hospital consultants* in Phase Two sites (most items used five-point rating scales with space for additional comments)

- Personal details.
- Current position and employment history.
- Practice in treatment of women under 18 years (discussion of options, arrangements for antenatal clinics, any special provision for women aged under 18 years – named midwife, maternity social worker, dedicated antenatal classes, special provision for mothers when they leave hospital, etc.).
- Perceptions of quality of local services for young mothers and young women who choose to terminate.
- Nature of service provision locally.
- Routes of access.
- Personal views on abortion.
- Upper time limits for procedure.
- Whether local provision is limited by waiting times; what are the average waiting times?
- Any special arrangements for under 16 year olds.
- Personal willingness to accept consent without parent/guardian being informed.
- Preferred aftercare arrangements for young mothers.
- Perceptions of barriers to providing better service.
- Personal views on whether young women should be provided with NHS abortion services.

Appendix 3

Phase Three data collection

Topics covered in interviews with *young women* in Phase Three sites
- Personal background details (family, living arrangements, education, religious involvement, ethnicity, etc.).
- Prior views on ideal age to become a mother.
- Prior opinions about abortion.
- Perceived influences on views.
- Events leading up to pregnancy (relationship status, contraceptive use).
- Circumstances of pregnancy (partner relationship, contraception use).
- Details of decision-making process (who discussed with, their views, who influenced decision, etc.).
- Eventual decision and reasons.
- Feelings about events and decision.
- If abortion, describe process of referral and procedure, and feelings.
- If maternity, describe process and feelings.
- Comments on care received.
- Views on abortion post-event.
- Any regrets and/or positive feelings about decision taken.

Topics covered in interviews with *older community members* in Phase Three sites
- Personal details (age, ethnicity, occupation, religion, pregnancy history, relationship history, etc.).
- Views on abortion generally and historical changes in attitudes.
- View on abortion provision and funding.
- Perceived influences on views.
- Best age to have child.
- Views on responsibility for teenage pregnancy.
- Changing times and norms concerning teenage sexuality and pregnancy.
- Views on provision for teenage mothers.
- Views on sex education.
- Professionals and confidentiality.
- How would/did they react if own child had teenage conception?
- Perceptions of local community and teenage pregnancy issues.
- Views on extent of 'problem' and ways of dealing with it.

Topics covered on questionnaire for *general practitioners* in Phase Three sites (most items used five-point rating scales with space for additional comments)

- Personal details.
- Views on extent to which pregnant young women under 18 are well provided for locally if (a) they choose to continue and (b) choose to terminate (separately for three trimesters).
- Views on whether young women under 18 should be provided with NHS procedure.
- Whether free pregnancy testings are provided on request at their practice and, if so, whether this is advertised.
- How many pregnant women aged under 18 they see each year, on average.
- The proportion of these who opt to continue their pregnancy.
- Procedures for pregnant young women who seem (a) sure and (b) unsure about what they want to do.
- Use of any other professionals in process.
- Assessment of quality of referral routes for abortion services locally for young women aged under 18.
- Whether they personally refer women under 18 for termination of pregnancy procedures under the provisions of the Abortion Act and, if not, why not.
- In their recent experience, what is the average waiting time for women under 18, (a) between referral and assessment and (b) between assessment and procedure?
- How women aged under 18 obtain assessment for abortion in their area.
- Views on factors that lead to difficulties.
- Whether they refer for abortions *under 16s* who refuse to inform their parents or guardians?
- Care of under-16s in practice.
- Whether practice has a written policy on confidentiality for young people and, if so, is it, and how is it, advertised?
- Perceptions of views of abortion in local community.

Table A3.1 Termination sample

Respondent	Age at event	Age at interview	Relationship status at conception	Relationship status at interview	Other pregnancies[a]	Ethnic group	Social dep score[b]
TOP1	16	19	Single	Married	2 (16, 18) post TOP, both continued	White British	−1.58
TOP2	14	14	Single	Single	None	White British	5.71
TOP3	16	16	Single, boyfriend	Single, boyfriend	None	White British	3.63
TOP4	17	20	Single	Single	1 (18) continued	White British	−1.48
TOP5	17	19	Single, boyfriend	Single	None	White British	
TOP6	16	16	Single, partner	Single, partner	None	White British	
TOP7	16	16	Single, boyfriend	Single, boyfriend	None	White British	
TOP8	17	20	Single, boyfriend	Single	1 (17) post TOP, continued	White British	
TOP9	17	17	Single	Single	1 (14) planned to continue, miscarried	White British	2.11
TOP10	17	19	Single, partner	Engaged	1 (19) aborted	Turkish	
TOP11	16	19	Single, boyfriend	Single	None	White British	−1.22
TOP12	17	18	Single	Single	None	White British	0.56
TOP13	16	18	Single, cohabiting	Single, cohabiting	1 (18) aborted	Mixed race	6.13
TOP14	15	16	Single	Single	None	White, British	6.13
TOP15	16	18	Single, boyfriend	Single	1 (13) continued	Black African	
TOP16	17	22	Single, cohabiting	Single, cohabiting	2 (15, 17) both continued	White British	
TOP17	16	23	Single, boyfriend	Single, partner	2 (18, 19) both continued	White British	
TOP18	15	15	Single	Single	None	White British	6.73
TOP19	17	18	Single, boyfriend	Single	None	White British	3.87
TOP20	16	17	Single, boyfriend	Single, boyfriend	One (17) aborted	Pakistani	−2.14
TOP21	17	17	Single	Single	2 (14 aborted, 15 continued)	White British	3.78
TOP22	16	16	Single, boyfriend	Single, boyfriend	None	White British	6.12
TOP23	17	17	Single	Single	None	White British	6.84
TOP24	15	16	Single	Single, boyfriend	1 (15 before TOP) continued	White British	
TOP25	17	23	Single, boyfriend	Engaged	None	White British	
TOP26	17	22	Single, boyfriend	Single	None	White British	

a Pregnancy history – first number refers to number of additional pregnancies, followed by age at conception and outcome.

b Social deprivation score for ward of residence at time of interview for those respondents who provided full postcode; a higher positive score indicates a greater level of social deprivation in that ward.

Table A3.1 Termination sample continued

Respondent	Age at event	Age at interview	Relationship status at conception	Relationship status at interview	Other pregnancies[a]	Ethnic group	Social dep score[b]
TOP27	16	23	Single	Single, boyfriend	None	White British	
TOP28	17	20	Single, boyfriend	Single, boyfriend	None	White British	
TOP29	17	21	Single, boyfriend	Single, boyfriend	None	White British	
TOP30	17	21	Single, boyfriend	Single, boyfriend	None	White British	
TOP31	14	18	Single, boyfriend	Single	1 (16) planned to continue, miscarried	White British	
TOP32	17	17	Single, boyfriend	Single, boyfriend	None	White British	
TOP33	17	22	Single, boyfriend	Single, boyfriend	None	White British	
TOP34	17	21	Single	Single	2 (17 aborted, 18 continued) post TOP	White British	
TOP35	16	22	Single, boyfriend	Single	None	British	−2.58
TOP36	17	22	Single, partner	Single	None	British	
TOP37	16	21	Single, boyfriend	Single, boyfriend	None	White British	
TOP38	15	15	Single, boyfriend	Single, boyfriend	None	White British	0.56
TOP39	17	17	Single, partner	Single, partner	None	White British	
TOP40	14	14	Single, boyfriend	Single	None	Mixed race	6.15
TOP41	17	17	Single, partner	Single, partner	None	White British	
TOP42	17	18	Single, boyfriend	Single	None	White British	0.99
TOP43	17	17	Single, boyfriend	Single, boyfriend	None	White British	7.59
TOP44	15	15	Single, boyfriend	Single, boyfriend	None	White British	1.28
TOP45	17	21	Single	Single, boyfriend	None	White British	
TOP46	15	24	Single, boyfriend	Single	3 (18 continued, 19 continued, 24 aborted)	White British	
TOP47	16	21	Single, boyfriend	Single, boyfriend	None	White British	
TOP48	17	18	Single, boyfriend	Single	None	White British	
TOP49	17	17	Single, boyfriend	Single, boyfriend	None	White European	7.21
TOP50	17	18	Single, boyfriend	Single	1 (18 aborted)	White British	1.0
TOP51	16	17	Single	Single	None	Mixed race	

a Pregnancy history – first number refers to number of additional pregnancies, followed by age at conception and outcome.

b Social deprivation score for ward of residence at time of interview for those respondents who provided full postcode; a higher positive score indicates a greater level of social deprivation in that ward.

Table A3.2 Maternity sample

Respondent	Age at event	Age at interview	Relationship status at conception	Relationship status at interview	Other pregnancies[a]	Ethnic group	Social dep score[b]
M1	16	16	Single, boyfriend	Single	None	White British	5.86
M2	16	17	Single	Single	None	White British	5.86
M3	16	17	Single	Single	None	White British	0.35
M4	17	18	Single partner	Single, partner	None	White British	-1.58
M5	17	17	Single	Single	None	White British	0.35
M6	17	17	Single, partner	Single, partner	None	White British	1.37
M7	15	17	Single, boyfriend	Single	None	White British	-1.58
M8	16	17	Single, partner	Single	None	White British	-0.13
M9	17	18	Single, boyfriend	Single	None	White British	-2.33
M10	14	16	Single, boyfriend	Single, boyfriend	None	White British	3.74
M11	15	16	Single	Single, boyfriend	None	White British	1.27
M12	16	19	Single, partner	Single	None	White British	
M13	16	20	Single, boyfriend	Single	None	White British	-1.48
M14	17	20	Single, boyfriend	Single	None	White British	-1.71
M15	17	20	Single, partner	Single, partner	1 (19) continued	White British	-1.48
M16	17	19	Single, partner	Single, partner	None	Mixed race	
M17	17	21	Single, partner	Married	2 (18, 20) continued	White British	
M18	16	20	Single, partner	Single	1 (19) continued	White British	
M19	15	16	Single, boyfriend	Single	None	White British	
M20	15	17	Single, boyfriend	Single, boyfriend	None	White British	
M21	16	17	Single, boyfriend	Single, boyfriend	None	White British	
M22	16	17	Single	Single	None	White British	
M23	14	15	Single, boyfriend	Single	None	White British	
M24	15	17	Single, boyfriend	Single, partner	None	White British	
M25	16	18	Single, boyfriend	Single	None	White British	
M26	17	18	Single	Single	None	White British	
M27	15	16	Single	Single	None	White British	

a Pregnancy history – first number refers to number of additional pregnancies, followed by age at conception and outcome.

b Social deprivation score for ward of residence at time of interview for those respondents who provided full postcode; a higher positive score indicates a greater level of social deprivation in that ward.